Cambridge Studies in Social Anthropology

GENERAL EDITOR: JACK GOODY
*William Wyse Professor of Social Anthropology
University of Cambridge*

Rethinking Symbolism

Cambridge Studies and Papers in Social Anthropology

STUDIES

R. G. ABRAHAMS, *The Political Organization of Unyamwezi*

S. J. TAMBIAH, *Buddhism and the Spirit Cults in North-east Thailand*

A. KUPER, *Kalahari Village Politics*

A. STRATHERN, *The Rope of Moka*

J. STAUDER, *The Majangir*

J. BUNNAG, *Buddhist Monk, Buddhist Layman*

E. N. GOODY, *Contexts of Kinship*

C. OPPONG, *Marriage among a Matrilineal Elite*

A. T. CARTER, *Elite Politics in Rural India*

V. MAHER, *Women and Property in Morocco*

D. SPERBER, *Rethinking Symbolism*

A. MACFARLANE, *Resources and Population*

J. G. PERISTIANY (ed.), *Mediterranean Family Structures*

PAPERS

J. GOODY (ed.), *The Developmental Cycle in Domestic Groups*

E. R. LEACH (ed.), *Aspects of Caste in South India, Ceylon and North-west Pakistan*

M. FORTES (ed.), *Marriage in Tribal Societies*

J. GOODY (ed.), *Succession to High Office*

E. R. LEACH (ed.), *Dialectic in Practical Religion*

A. RICHARDS and A. KUPER (eds.), *Councils in Action*

J. GOODY and S. J. TAMBIAH, *Bridewealth and Dowry*

Rethinking Symbolism

DAN SPERBER

TRANSLATED BY
ALICE L. MORTON

CAMBRIDGE UNIVERSITY PRESS

CAMBRIDGE

LONDON · NEW YORK · MELBOURNE

HERMANN, PUBLISHERS IN ARTS AND SCIENCE

PARIS

Published by the Syndics of the Cambridge University Press
The Pitt Building, Trumpington Street, Cambridge CB2 1RP
Bentley House, 200 Euston Road, London NW1 2DB
32 East 57th Street, New York, NY 10022, USA
296 Beaconsfield Parade, Middle Park, Melbourne 3206, Australia

ISBN 2 7056 5787 8 (Hermann)

© 1974, Hermann, 293 rue Lecourbe, 75015 Paris
© in the English language edition, Cambridge University Press 1975

Cambridge University Press ISBNs:
0 521 20834 3 hard covers
0 521 09967 6 paperback

First published in English translation 1975

Printed in France

To Deirdre Wilson

Table of Contents

Preface   x

1 SYMBOLISM AND LANGUAGE

The rationalist criterion   1
The semiological criterion   4
Is symbolism a code?   12

2 HIDDEN MEANINGS

Limits of exegesis   17
The cryptological view   23
The Freudian view   34
All keys to symbols must themselves be symbolically
    interpreted   47

3 ABSENT MEANING

The structuralist view   51
The model: oppositions and inversions   59
Methodological interpretation   63
Theoretical interpretation   68
The model: transformations of myths   72
Interpretation: mythology is not a language   79
Lévi-Strauss and the end of semiology   83

4 SYMBOLISM AND KNOWLEDGE

The learning of symbolism   85
Symbolic knowledge and encyclopaedic knowledge   91

CONTENTS

Beliefs and figures   101
Symbolism is knowledge about knowledge   107
Symbolicity is a property of conceptual representa-
tions   110

5 THE SYMBOLIC MECHANISM

Smells and individual symbolism   115
Focalisation and evocation   119
Irony and verbal symbolism   123
Christian leopards and were-hyenas: cultural sym-
bolism   129
Principles and forms of symbolic work   140
Symbolism in general   146

References   151

Translator's Note

It may be noted that several passages in the present translation do not correspond exactly to the French text. The reason for this is that, after the translation had been completed, the author made certain changes in the English version which he deemed necessary to render his thoughts more precise.

A.L.M.

Preface

What is a theory of symbolism? What conditions must it fulfil? What general properties must it account for? In this book, I propose an answer to these questions. The notion of symbolism itself will not be defined, but only circumscribed in the course of the argument: it will be shown how a set of diverse phenomena (from myths to linguistic figures, from religious rituals to the gestures of courtesy) may be approached in the same way.

This work is informed by a view of anthropology that I state briefly without additional justification: human learning abilities are phylogenetically determined and culturally determinant. They are determined in the same way for all members of the species; they do not therefore determine cultural *variations* but only cultural *variability*. Cultural variability is at once made possible and constrained by human learning ability. Anthropology has as its object this possibility and these constraints.

In this perspective, the most interesting cultural knowledge is tacit knowledge – that is to say, that which is not made explicit. When those who have this knowledge are able to make it explicit, I shall speak of implicit knowledge. When they are incapable of this, I shall speak of unconscious knowledge. Explicit and expressly-imparted knowledge may in principle be learned by rote, and it is therefore only direct evidence of the quantitative limits of human learning ability. Conversely, tacit knowledge may in no case be acquired by rote; it must be reconstructed by each individual;

it is therefore direct evidence of specific learning abilities, of a qualitatively determined creative competence.

For the study of tacit knowledge the basic data are intuitions, they are the judgments that the members of a cultural group systematically express without elaborating on the underlying argument. For example, the members of a society agree that a given phrase is insulting in a given situation, but they are incapable of defining entirely the criteria on which their judgment rests. Explicit cultural knowledge makes sense only in as much as it is the object of an underlying tacit knowledge. Thus proverbs, whose statement is part of explicit cultural knowledge, are the object on the one hand of a generally implicit gloss; on the other, of an unconscious knowledge that determines the exact conditions in which their use is appropriate, and the symbolic nuances it is proper to bring to their interpretation. The task of the ethnographer is to explicate this sort of tacit knowledge. The task of the anthropologist is to explain what makes it possible – that is to say, to describe the universal conditions of its learning.

Symbolism is paradigmatic in this respect, for its explicit forms are unintelligible by themselves and their study has always presupposed the existence of an underlying tacit knowledge. But what is the nature of this knowledge and what is its relationship to explicitness? The most generally accepted answer is the following: the explicit forms of symbolism are *signifiants* (signifiers) associated to tacit *signifiés* (signifieds) as in the model of the relationships between sound and meaning in language. In the first three chapters, I argue against this semiological view. In the last two, I develop a cognitive view and show in particular that symbolic interpretation is not a matter of decoding, but an improvisation that rests on an implicit knowledge and obeys unconscious rules.

By asserting that symbolism is a cognitive mechanism,

I mean that it is an autonomous mechanism that, alongside the perceptual and conceptual mechanisms, participates in the construction of knowledge and in the functioning of the memory. On this point I differ from semiological approaches which see symbolism above all as an instrument of social communication. Indeed – as we shall see – symbolism plays a major role in social communication, but this is not a constitutive function of symbolism which would allow the prediction of its structure.

Further, I suggest as a possible hypothesis that the basic principles of the symbolic mechanism are not induced from experience but are, on the contrary, part of the innate mental equipment that makes experience possible. On this point, I differ from behaviourism in psychology and cultural relativism in anthropology (or at least from their most dogmatic forms), two views according to which not only knowledge, but also the principles of its organisation, are uniquely determined by experience. These views are based on unjustifiable *a priori* assumptions. If the general principles of symbolism are in fact as I describe them, it is not clear what, in experience or in instruction, would determine their acquisition; the hypothesis of their innateness is therefore in no way implausible.

I have not tried to write an erudite work and the reader will not find here any history of theories of symbolism. Many important authors are not even mentioned and at least one – Sigmund Freud – is only cited for a minimal and marginal part of his contribution to the study of symbolism. I have used the views of my predecessors when it seemed useful to discuss them without, however, trying to do justice to them; nor have I tried to analyse in depth the concrete examples that I use as illustrations. This is particularly true of the data borrowed from the culture of the Dorze of southern Ethiopia whose guest I was.* These data will be treated in a more detailed manner in another work.

I have not tried to construct a formally rigorous argument. In particular the considerations of logic, of linguistics and of psychology that enter into the development are simplified. The specialised reader may check for himself whether more rigorous presentation would have strengthened or weakened the argument or whether, as I believe, it would merely have made its exposition less digestible. An argument is only as strong as its weakest parts, which in this instance are those that are specifically anthropological. This state of affairs reflects as much my own insufficiencies as the embryonic nature of theoretical anthropology.

I wish to express my gratitude to those who have encouraged me, criticised me, and advised me in the course of this work, to Ginette Baty, Pierre Berès, François Dell, Marcel Detienne, Remo Guidieri, Jean Mettas, David Sapir, Pierre Smith, Jenka and Manès Sperber, Tzvetan Todorov, Terence Turner, Danièle Van de Velde and Deirdre Wilson.

---

* The Dorze are a group of about 20,000 persons speaking an Ometo dialect. They live in Ethiopia in the Gamo Highlands, west of the Rift Valley, at the level of Lake Abaya. They practise the culture of cereals and of *ensete edulis*, some animal husbandry and especially the weaving that has made them famous in their own country. They are organised in fourteen districts governed by assemblies and in about forty non-localised, exogamous patriclans. Their politico-ritual institutions may be divided into two groups: the one is based on the genealogical seniority of a hierarchy of permanent sacrificers; the other is based on individual accomplishment sanctioned by very elaborate *rites de passage* and by accession to honorific titles and to temporary positions. The big sacrificers (*demutsa*) and the dignitaries (*halak'a*) who are discussed in what follows relate respectively to the first and to the second groups of institutions (cf. Sperber 1974).

1

Symbolism and Language

Two criteria have, by turns, served to delimit the field of symbolism. According to the first criterion, the symbolic is the mental minus the rational; according to the second, it is the semiotic minus language. In one case as in the other, it is a residue.

The criterion of irrationality – today out of fashion – was elaborated principally in two ways. In the view of a Tylor or of a Frazer, primitive beliefs are the fruit of defective reasoning, of illicit inferences from insufficient data. Thus, according to Tylor, primitive man reflecting on dream experience, would have inferred from it the notion of a non-material entity – the soul – and would then have attributed this to other beings, animals or even inanimate objects, finally to lend it an existence independent of all material support, in the form of spirits. According to Frazer, magic had two forms, homeopathic and contagious, based on the confusion of similarity on the one hand, and contiguity on the other, with effective causality. Beliefs, with the practices based on them, would therefore be a set of errors resulting from insufficient rationality.

According to the second rationalist view, whose most prominent defender remains Lucien Lévy-Bruhl (even though he himself criticised it at the end of his life; see his *Carnets*, 1949), primitive beliefs were not the product of a failed rationality, but that of a mental activity that turns its back on the basic principle of all rationality – that of non-contradiction. Totemism, in which the fact that an individual

1

belongs to the human species does not for all that exclude his belonging simultaneously to an animal species, does not arise from a faulty application of the principle of identity, but from the consistent application of a principle of participation.

According to the first view, primitive man in his beliefs tries to be rational, but he fails to be systematic; according to the second, he is systematic, but does not try to be rational. Yet the very notion of the primitive that these two opposed views tended to develop has meanwhile dissolved, and with it the theory of a dinosaur-symbolism, a set of means of expression and of action adapted to conditions of a prattling humanity, but irrational in view of our present means and condemned already to microfilms: the dinosaur is alive and well.

The vigour of symbolism in our own culture, and the undoubted presence of rational thought in all societies, certainly weakens the conception of a primitive humanity irrational, either by insufficiency or by system; they do not for all that weaken the conception of an irrational symbolism.

The objection lies elsewhere: the rationalist view overdoes it more by a lack of elaboration than by a faulty elaboration. To study symbolism is to postulate that it is a system and to look for the principles that govern it. To assert that the principles of rationality enter into it insufficiently or not at all would only be interesting if rationality itself were defined, and in any event would not constitute the definition of symbolism itself.

It is one thing to postulate the systematic character of symbolism, another to demonstrate it; one thing to reject in principle the criterion of irrationality, another to dispense with it.

I am among the Dorze of southern Ethiopia and I am studying their symbolism. Someone explains to me how to cultivate fields. I listen with a distracted ear. Someone tells me that if the head of the family does not himself sow the first seeds, the harvest will be bad. This I note immediately.

I observe the comings and goings of the market; the spectacle is agreeable and I dream of the market of the Rue Mouffetard. Along comes a group of dignitaries who ignore the merchants and who undertake a circling of the market place in an anticlockwise direction. I enquire: the tour cannot be done in the other direction. Why? It is the custom. But then? One turns in the direction of the sun. How is that? Well, from right to left. I bombard my informants with questions.

My assistant says he is tired in the middle of the afternoon and goes to lie down. What a waste of time! He awakes, feels bad, and suspects the evil eye. Not such a waste after all.

Why is it that this bores, distracts or irritates me while that interests, concerns and delights me? I know that the genealogical position of the sower does not affect the germination of grain; that there are no more reasons, between the Tropic of Cancer and the Equator, for thinking that the sun turns from right to left rather than from left to right; that to turn 'like the sun' leaves the sun completely indifferent; that to circle the market and come back to one's point of departure without buying anything, or selling anything, saying or hearing anything, is not economical; and that, finally, the evil eye doesn't exist. Or to take still another example, when a Dorze friend says to me that pregnancy lasts nine months, I think, 'Good, they know that.' When he adds, 'but in some clans it lasts eight or ten months', I think, 'That's symbolic.' Why? Because it is false.

This needs clarification. Not all errors immediately strike me as symbolic, nor all symbolic discourse as necessarily erroneous. If, for example, instead of telling me that the stars are very small, the Dorze told me that they were larger than the earth, that some are perhaps inhabited, etc., then and then only do I scent symbolism. The economics of

3

error does not differ essentially from that of valid inference. Both try to account for a maximum of data by means of a minimum of hypotheses, and are capable of being falsified; the intellectual effort whether it succeeds or fails is rationally proportionate to its end, which is knowledge. Symbolic discourse, on the contrary, ignores this economics; it only retains from experience a minimum of fragments to establish a maximum of hypotheses, without caring to put them to the test; if its end is knowledge, then the intellectual effort expended is disproportionate and poorly applied.

I note then as symbolic all activity where the means put into play seem to me to be clearly disproportionate to the explicit or implicit end, whether this end be knowledge, communication or production – that is to say, all activity whose rationale escapes me. In short, the criterion I use in the field is in fact one of irrationality. I don't know that other anthropologists proceed differently.

There are thus three possibilities: either the criterion of irrationality is worthless and thinking we are delimiting the field of symbolism we are only gathering the bric-à-brac of our ignorance; or else, as mystical minds would have it, the criterion of irrationality is the right one, and symbolism is not open to scientific investigation; or else the criterion of irrationality delimits symbolism – albeit approximately – without for all that defining it, which will require explanation.

The second criterion – that symbolism is the semiotic minus language – seems to displace the first. Indeed, it is said, there is no irrational symbolism, there is only poorly-interpreted symbolism. This faulty interpretation is the first to come to the mind of a stranger to a society, and therefore to its symbolism. It seems irrational; it is only superficial. In fact, besides their manifest meaning or aim, symbolic phenomena have a hidden meaning.

In this view, symbolism does not have its own signals; it uses as signals signs already established elsewhere. One therefore has a sign – i.e. a signal plus an associated standard meaning (a *signifiant* plus a *signifié*) – which is itself related as a signal to an associated symbolic meaning. The mistake consists in taking the standard meaning which here is only an aspect of the signal, for the symbolic meaning which alone is relevant. Symbolism is a system of signs and as such – like language properly speaking – is a matter for semiology. But while language has its own signals which are only defined by their reciprocal articulation and their relation to linguistic meaning, symbolism uses as signals elements, acts or utterances that exist, and are also interpreted, independent of it.

Thus a myth at first seems like ordinary discourse. For one who knows the language in which it is narrated, it is not more difficult to paraphrase than is any other story, and its interpretation does not pose any particular linguistic problem. But this linguistic interpretation does not exhaust its meaning; rather it constitutes a complex signal that must become the object of a second interpretation, this time a symbolic one. The overt and often absurd sense of a myth is only an instrument of symbolic meaning.

Cults devoted to the gods of a pantheon seem at first glance to be homage rendered to supernatural beings of which nothing in experience rationally attests the existence. But a symbolic interpretation would show, for example (à la Dumézil) that these gods function as signals which in their reciprocal relations have for meaning a set of categories by means of which men represent to themselves their own society.

Many more examples could be taken from the theory of tropes, from the theory of dreams, from the anthropological, psychoanalytic, or semiological literature. There is no doubt that this perspective has made it possible to understand numerous institutions, to raise numerous problems, and to suggest numerous hypotheses. But it would be wrong to believe for all this that the semiotic nature of symbolism had ever been demonstrated.

It is with symbols as it is with spirits. If spirits speak by causing tables to turn, they don't – for all that – have much to say. If symbols mean, what they mean is almost always banal. The existence of spirits and the luxuriance of symbols are more fascinating than are their feeble messages about the weather.

If, for example, we interpret in the manner of Malinowski (1926) a myth of the origin of humanity, a rich and complex one telling of miraculous births and other unlikely events, as meaning that some particular clan has a right to privileges that it in fact exercises, we pose more problems than we resolve. The story means this right, or demonstrates it. If it means it, what needs explaining, surely, is why one was not content to state it (so many societies stick with 'it is the custom', 'it is the ancestors who decided it should be this way', etc.), why one invoked a long, complicated and obscure discourse. In turn, if the mythical narrative demonstrates the right, then belief in its truthfulness plays a fundamental role, and the problem of irrationality is only more clearly posed: not only must the unlikely be taken as true, but further, between the narrative interpretation and the symbolic one there is established a deductive relationship which lacks the generalisability which would make it logically admissible.

The criticism would be even sharper should it apply not only to the disappointing theory of Malinowski but also to the richest and most intuitively satisfying interpretation ever given of mythology, that of Claude Lévi-Strauss.

If myths have a symbolic meaning, the propositions expressed by this meaning may be of two varieties: synthetic or analytic; that is to say, about the world of experience or about the categories of thought. While his predecessors saw in the symbolic content of myths the expression of several banalities about the natural world or about society, Lévi-Strauss was the first systematically to explore the second possibility. The ordinary use of language utilises categories to make statements about the world. Symbolic thought, on the contrary, utilises statements about the world to establish relations between categories. Thus, any element of myth becomes relevant as soon as there is at least one other element with which it is in a relation of synonymy, of entailment, or of contradiction. The set of these analytic relations constitutes, if not the totality, at least the essence of the symbolic interpretation of myth.

In the Malinowskian view, myth is too rich with respect to its interpretation and this redundancy remains unexplained. In the Lévi-Straussian view, the redundancy of the signal (the mythic narrative) with respect to the meaning (the symbolic interpretation) does not seem to exceed the level indispensable to the functioning of all systems of signs. But the internal redundancy of the symbolic interpretation is extreme; the same relations between categories are gone over again and again.

Either the system of categories analysed and re-analysed throughout myths is a subsystem of the categories of language, and in this case it is hard to see what symbolic discourse adds – very expensively – to that which any speaker already knows and can explain much more simply; or else symbolic categories constitute a proper language and this language only speaks of itself. I know very well that the idea of a language which only speaks of itself has won over many of my contemporaries, but I admit being on my part insensible to its charms, and only finding in it a further difficult problem, in any event when it is a question of a product of human evolution.

The disproportion between means and end, clear in the

case of mythology, becomes truly exorbitant in the case of ritual. When we think of the time, the tension, the passion, and the expense necessary to put on the smallest ritual, how can we believe that the uncertain attribution of a semantic interpretation – one therefore paraphrasable in ordinary language at a comparatively non-existent expense of energy – can account in any fashion for the nature of the phenomenon? The argument according to which the redundancy of a symbolic message gives it a force of conviction that the simple linguistic message lacks, only begs the question. Redundancy alone creates lassitude more than conviction.

The semiological view of symbolism therefore does not eliminate the problem of irrationality, it only shifts it. The apparent irrationality of symbolism does not arise from an error of appreciation of facts or from faulty reasoning, but from a disproportion between the means put into play and the avowed or supposed ends: those ends do not rationally explain these means. Yet, precisely, following the semiological view, symbolism puts into play considerable means of expression to express platitudes or to reiterate plays on words...

So far, I have tried to show that the view according to which symbolic phenomena would have their own meaning eludes but does not solve the problem of irrationality. There is worse yet: can one usefully say that symbols mean?

The word 'meaning' has so many meanings that it always fits in somehow. It is said indifferently that the word 'moon' means the moon, that 'Hear, hear!' means approval, that fever means illness, and that the election of the new president means nothing good. Meaning and reference, meaning and connotation, meaning and diagnosis, meaning and prognosis, are confused. But what may be confused harmlessly in ordinary speech should be carefully distinguished in philosophical or scientific exposition. Especially in the latter one should not introduce the notion of meaning without having sufficiently circumscribed it, having shown that it is relevant and that it leads to better work.

The only discipline in which the notion of meaning fulfils these conditions (and then not always) is linguistics. Consider for example the following sentences:

1 (a) I like Juliette more than I like Justine.
(b) I like Juliette more than Justine does.
(c) I like Juliette more than Justine.
2 (a) Joseph is my aunt's husband.
(b) Joseph is my uncle.
(c) My aunt's husband is my uncle.
3 (a) Joseph is my aunt's husband.
(b) Joseph is single.
(c) My aunt's husband is single.

Any English speaker, without knowing anything either about the people spoken of, or about the speaker, knows that one cannot assert (1a) and deny (1c), nor assert (1b) and deny (1c); that one can assert (1c) and deny either (1a) and (1b) but not both at once. He therefore knows that (1c) has two meanings of which (1a) and (1b) are respectively paraphrases. He knows that one cannot assert (2a) and deny (2b) or, which comes to the same thing, that (2c) is true by virtue of its meaning alone; it is an analytic tautology. Further, he knows that one cannot simultaneously assert (3a) and (3b) or, which comes to the same thing, that (3c) is false by virtue of its meaning alone; it is an analytic contradiction.

A theory of language must take account of this type of intuition shared by all speakers. These intuitions are about relations between sentences or between phrases. The existence of these systematic relations justifies the adoption of a theoretical concept, that of meaning. Just as the notion of temperature, used in current language as if it designated a perceptible aspect of things, only takes on an exact and useful sense if one refers it, for example, to the relation between

9

the variable height of a column of mercury and a fixed scale that serves to measure that height, so the notion of meaning only acquires scientific status in referring to intuitively perceived relations between signs – that is to say in particular those of paraphrase or of analyticity; to describe the meaning of a sentence (or of a phrase) is merely to give the means of identifying these relations.

For two sentences no longer to be considered as paraphrases, or two phrases as synonyms, it suffices that there be a context in which, when one is substituted for the other, the truth-value is affected. Thus, 'my uncle' and 'my aunt's husband', phrases that are equivalent in a large number of contexts, are no longer equivalent in the following cases:

4 (a) My uncle is single.
(b) My aunt's husband is single.

(4b) is contradictory, while the truth value of (4a) depends on the civil state.

For a sentence no longer to be considered as analytic, it suffices to conceive of two worlds in which its truth-value changes without its meaning being affected. Thus 'The horse is an animal' is true in all worlds, even in a world in which there are no horses (cf. 'the unicorn is an animal'), while 'the horse is a domesticated animal' would not be true in a world in which all horses were wild. In short, the paraphrase must not affect the truth-value of the context in which it is inserted, and the context must not affect the truth-value of the tautology or of the analytic contradiction.

The positing of such conditions for the interpretation and use of the notion of meaning is in no way arbitrary. They are motivated by the necessity of adequately describing the systematic intuitions of speakers. There are available other intuitions about sentences that ordinary language also describes in terms of meaning. Thus the contradiction 'My aunt's husband is single' could be understood as meaning to say that my aunt is away on a trip. But, if we wish to analyse this interpretation, we would be wrong in postulating a second meaning for 'is single' which would be 'whose wife is away'. In this case, on the one hand the ironical effect which must be accounted for would be completely lost and, on the other 'So-and-so is single' would never exclude that So-and-so might be married. None of the expressive effects of this sort can be analysed without taking into consideration the meaning, in the precise sense in which it has been defined, to show in what way it has been departed from. There are therefore in any event at least two very distinct notions, and for the sake of clarity they must be differently designated.

Without paraphrase and analyticity (and other relations intuitively perceived which I shall pass over; cf. J. J. Katz 1972), there is no meaning. Is there, therefore, paraphrase or analyticity in symbolism?

If symbolisation were a form of meaning that only differed from linguistic meaning by the type of signals it used and if the set of symbols (of a given culture) constituted a language, one should be able systematically to substitute certain simple or complex symbols for each symbol in all contexts as one can in language replace any word by a definition. Or else if we considered that symbols meant without, for all that, constituting a proper language, one should be able to substitute for them the verbal expression of their meaning (these substitutions, needless to say, not affecting the total sense). Anyone who has ever studied symbolic phenomena knows that their interpretation depends on the context and is generally modified by any substitution. Were there cases in which there were symbols whose interpretation was stable in all contexts, or contexts in which a substitution did not affect the total symbolic interpretation, when is it that – these two conditions both being satisfied – one could speak of synonymy or of paraphrase? This would in any event be the exception and not the rule, and meaning still could not be held to be intrinsic to symbolisation.

Imagine two myths to which the same interpretation is given – for example, that they found as rights the privileges of a clan. Would we then say of someone who recognised the truth of one myth and not that of the other that he contradicted himself? Or else that he only understood half of the symbolism of his culture? Certainly not; there is neither paraphrase between these myths nor, therefore, contradiction in these contrasting beliefs.

The view of Lévi-Strauss poses some more interesting problems. According to it, symbolic thought only incidentally expresses statements about the world and, instead, systematically explores the relations between categories. The problem of meaning therefore comes down to that of analyticity: it would suffice that the relations between categories expressed by symbolism be properly analytic for symbolism to have meaning. Yet the relations revealed by Lévi-Strauss are those of homology and not of paraphrase, of correspondence and not of tautology, of opposition and not of contradiction. This does not in any way lessen the interest of the relationships revealed; only they are not relations of meaning.

Many thought they had discovered the meaning of symbols, but none has linked the interpretation of his discoveries to the notion of meaning itself, neither to that suggested by the study of language, nor to any other that has been properly defined. If it is vain to analyse symbolism in terms of the model of language, it is still a temptation which scholars have escaped by first escaping from any care for precision.

Victor Turner, whose contribution to the study of symbolism is considerable, and whose care for conceptual precision is otherwise constant, writes: 'When we talk about the "meaning" of a symbol, we must be careful to distinguish between at least three levels or fields of meaning. These I propose to call: (1) the level of indigenous interpretation (or, briefly, exegetical meaning); (2) the operational meaning; and (3) the positional meaning' (Turner 1967: 50). The 'exegetical meaning' is given by the native commentary. The 'operational meaning' of a symbol is equivalent to its use and to the affective qualities linked to that use – 'aggressive, sad, penitent, joyful, derisive, and so on' (Turner 1967: 51). The 'positional meaning' derives from structural relationships that symbols have among themselves.

Exegetical meaning has three bases: a 'nominal' base that derives from associations with the name of the symbol; a 'substantial' base that derives from natural and material properties of objects used as symbols; finally an 'artifactual' base in the case of made symbols (see also Turner 1969*b*: 11–13).

This inventory of the properties of symbols that Turner develops and illustrates is undoubtedly useful; it underscores distinctions which are generally neglected. It is then all the more paradoxical to see, as the descriptive categories multiply and become refined, the concept of meaning become distended and take in indiscriminately all the conceivable properties of symbols, no matter how heterogeneous.

This laxity in the use of 'meaning' – particularly clear in Turner because it contrasts with a definite refinement in the use of other concepts – characterises as well the whole set of works devoted to symbolism. I wish to show that this laxity is not fortuitous and that it is in fact impossible to circumscribe the notion of meaning in such a way that it may still apply to the relationship between symbols and their interpretation.

If symbolism has no semantics comparable to that of language, we may still define meaning in a wider and nevertheless precise manner and see whether, in this new sense, symbols have meaning. Thus, I take the notion of meaning to include the relationship between message and interpretation such as is characteristic of all codes, even when these interpretations do not enter into analytic relationships proper to the semantics of natural languages.

A code is a set of pairs (message, interpretation) given either, as in an elementary case such as that of Morse code, in the form of a simple list, or in more complex cases, for example cartomancy and, of course, language, in the form of rules that potentially define all the pairs of the code, and those alone. It is not necessary in this broad definition that the relationships message-interpretation be one – one; in other words, several interpretations may correspond to the same message, and vice versa.

A code may underlie both a coding device and a decoding device. When such a device associates an input to an output (a messege to an interpretation or the inverse), it treats it as a particular occurrence of a phenomenon of which it already has the potential representation. Analysing the input then comes down to recognition, and the association with the output is a matter of reconstruction.

The subsequent processing of the information is done on the output of such a device. Thus, when it is a question of emitting a message, the interpretation – once coded – plays no further role; the message is substituted for it – the telegraphist substitutes for a text in ordinary language a series of Morse signals and it is these signals, not the text, that are transmitted. Similarly, a received message, once completely interpreted, is no longer the object of any processing; it is the interpretation substituted for it that will be processed – it is the predictions of cartomancy and not the cards thrown that give food for thought. Or again, if the meaning of things heard is unmistakable, it is the semantic interpretation and not the phonetic message that will be kept in mind.

All pairing is not necessarily encoding; the instructions on a packet of washing powder or a medicine label are not substituted for the content of the bottle or of the packet; nor is the price tag substituted for the object on sale. True, these are fixed pairs, but not the (message, interpretation) pairs. Inversely, information may be interpreted without that interpretation being associated with it in a stable pair, and therefore without that interpretation constituting a decoding. If, for example, hearing a piece of music, I associate with it a reverie that for me constitutes the 'meaning' of it, I do not, in doing so, reconstruct the pairs of a pre-given code; rather I give myself over to mental improvisation.

There is no doubt that symbolic phenomena are regularly paired to commentaries, to proper uses, to other symbolic phenomena, as Turner has noted. Nor is there any doubt that symbolic phenomena are interpreted. The problem is to know whether the phenomena paired to symbols constitute interpretations of them, and whether the interpretations of symbols are regularly paired to them. It is this that all semiological views of symbolism must assert.

To extend the notion of meaning to that of encoding, and to say that symbols mean in this sense, is to give to the semiological view the most vague interpretation, the least specific one possible. It is to assert simply that to each symbol corresponds a fixed set of interpretations, that to each interpretation corresponds a fixed set of symbols or, in other terms, that a particular occurrence of a symbol selects certain pairs (symbol, interpretation) among a set defined in the very structure of symbolism. If at least this is not asserted, to say that symbols mean, or to say that symbolism comes under the heading of semiology, is to say nothing at all. For then not only symbols, not only sentences, but all objects of perception and of thought may as well be said to mean; and not only symbolics, not only linguistics, but all the sciences may be considered as branches of a semiology so distended that it loses all value.

Starting with the notion of meaning extended to all codes,

one may question oneself at leisure about the particular structure of symbolic codes. The conceivable models are indefinitely varied, so weak is the hypothesis about the semiological nature of symbolism when formulated in this way. Yet it is still much too strong. The one single condition that would permit the consideration of symbolism as a code is not fulfilled: no list gives, no rule generates, a set of pairs (symbol, interpretation) such that each occurrence of a symbol finds in it its prefigured treatment. Here I run up not only against the postulate of many scholars, but even against the common sense that knows a transitive verb 'to symbolise', and for which it is necessary that symbols symbolise something. Yes, but what?

As soon as the question is posed, common sense hesitates, replies negligently or neglects to reply, and abandons the scholar to his explorations. It is clear in any case that no explicit or implicit shared knowledge permits the attribution to each symbol of its interpretations, to each interpretation its symbols, in short to postulate a set of pairs from which then to abstract the structure. In these conditions, the semiological hypotheses are less about the structure of the symbolic code than about what would constitute its bits and pieces.

The semiologist, not at all discouraged, looks for what symbols symbolise, and since the answer is neither in the field of his intuition nor in that of his perception, it must be that it is hidden: either one hides it or it hides itself. Whence come the only two possible semiological views: cryptological symbolism or unconscious symbolism. In the next chapter I examine these two views and, in particular, the manner in which Victor Turner on the one hand, and Sigmund Freud on the other, have developed them. I show that the facts they have brought to light do not justify a semiological view of symbolism. In the following chapter, I show that Lévi-Strauss' view is not really semiological anyhow.

2
Hidden Meanings

In the field, the ethnographer quickly discovers many phenomena he judges to be symbolic. He questions his hosts, and asks them to explain. Three things can happen.

In the first case, the informants reply, 'It is the custom', 'We have always done it that way', 'Our ancestors knew the meaning of these things, but we have forgotten it.' The ethnographer sadly imagines that he has come too late, that in the era of the ancestors, they would have known how to answer him. Generally, it does not occur to him that the ancestors had their ancestors, and perhaps they too believed they had forgotten. But the ethnographer does not willingly resign himself. Scraps of this knowledge must persist and he continues to ask, sometimes to the point at which his informants, to rid themselves of the intruder, answer him – no matter what.

I learned, in Dorze, that when a young man marries, his father builds him a hut against the fence of his compound and plants in front of it a shrub called *oloma*. An informant, full of kindness, and seeing that I was pained by his 'It is the custom', added more or less this: the *oloma* is a vigorous plant which buds a good deal and which transplants readily. And – did he say it? did I hear it? – these properties have something to do with the fertility one wishes for the new couple. I thought I thus held the key to a symbol; data gathered afterwards forced me to change my tune. One also plants an *oloma* when establishing a foreigner on one's land, without which he could not slaughter a domestic animal either for a sacrifice or for an ordinary meal.

As informants emphasised, the two situations have something in common but something which has nothing to do with fertility: it is taboo to copulate, it is taboo to slaughter a beast, on the lands of a senior or of a non-kinsman unless an *oloma*, planted by the owner of the area, lifts the prohibition. Thus, what we have is the ritual neutralisation of a space. But what is it that makes this plant particularly apposite to play that role? I am not sure; perhaps the fact that it often grows in the hedgerows that border roads, that is to say, in a liminal space which, when ritually planted, it recreates. And what does the *oloma* mean? I haven't a clue, and I doubt that there is anything at all there to be known.

In a general way, the Dorze, who utilise a large number of symbols in connection with multiple, lively and complex rituals, do not explain them, and restrict their comments to the rules of use. Transition rituals are not accompanied by any initiation into a body of esoteric knowledge. The few bits of exegesis that I gathered were improvised by good-natured informants in response to questions that no Dorze would have dreamed of asking. Doubtless, when an ethnographer asserts that such and such a type of knowledge is not to be found among the people he has studied, it may be that he has done his work badly. However, the Dorze situation resembles that encountered by many ethnographers. All this goes to show that a complex symbolic system can work very well without being accompanied by any exegetic commentary.

In another case, the ethnographer discovers that if most informants do not answer his questions there are still some experts who know how to explain symbols. He must find them, conquer them and, if necessary, have himself initiated.

Thus, Victor Turner's research on the symbolism of the Ndembu of Zambia took on a different dimension from the day when he met a certain Mushona, called The Hornet. Turner has admirably described this encounter and portrayed the character (Turner 1967). He was walking with his assistant along a path when an 'elderly gnome' (1967: 131) came to join them. Learning that he was a 'doctor', Turner asked him 'the meaning of some of the medicines [he] had seen doctors handle' (Turner 1967: 132). Mushona replied readily at length concerning the symbolic value of several plants that they encountered on the road. 'Now I had heard many other Ndembu interpret plant symbols before, but never so clearly and cogently as this. I was to become familiar with this mode of exposition. The swift-running commentary on unsolicited details, the parenthetical explanations, the vivid mimicry of ritual speech, and above all, the depth of psychological insight' (Turner 1967: 133).

Victor Turner was to work daily with Mushona over eight months. We would be mistaken in imagining that Mushona was content purely and simply to transmit a body of knowledge that he had himself received, to speak as he would have been able to do to another Ndembu: 'A new and exhilarating intellectual dimension had opened up to him as well as to myself in our discussions of symbolism... He delighted in making explicit what he had known subliminally about his own religion. A curious quirk of fate had brought him an audience and fellow enthusiast of a kind he could never have encountered in the villages' (Turner 1967: 138).

Mushona is a marginal in his own society. His interest in the exegesis of symbols extends far beyond that of other Ndembu, just as Turner's interest in this area far exceeds that of his colleagues. From their encounter emerged a body of work on symbolism of an exceptional richness.

If Mushona pushes further the exegetical dimension of symbolism, it is already present to a remarkable degree in Ndembu culture. 'In a *Ndembu* ritual context, almost every article used, every gesture employed, every song or prayer, every unit of space and time, by convention stands for something other than itself. It is more than it seems, and often a good deal more. The Ndembu are aware of the expressive or symbolic function of ritual elements. A ritual element or unit is called *chijikijilu*.' This word literally means a land-mark or a blaze used by hunters to find their path. A *chijikijilu* has 'a name (*ijina*) and it has an appearance (*chakulumbwishu*)' (Turner 1969*a*: 15).

For example, for the tree *museng'u* (*Ochna sp.*), 'the Ndembu derive the name of this species from *ku-seng'uka* "to multiply". The tree bears a great number of tiny black edible fruits, and informants connect this prolificity with its name. It is also connected with the term *ku-seng'ula* "to bless"... *Musengu* is used in both hunting and "gynecological" rites; in the former it represents "a multiplicity of kills", in the latter, "a multiplicity of offspring" ' (Turner 1967: 289).

This sort of symbolic knowledge is dispensed by the Ndembu on the occasion of particular rituals. When Mushona worked with Turner, he was accused by some of revealing secrets. Since these secrets were poorly guarded, the accu-sation was benign. Other societies push esotericism much further, as Griaule and his students found out among the Dogon of Mali.

Sometimes, on the other hand, the ethnographer easily finds answers to his questions. Symbols are so to speak given with their keys, and if some informants know more of them than others, the situation in this respect does not differ from that which one encounters in studying kinship, econ-omics, history, etc. Thus, in Christian countries, no one is unaware of what the Cross represents, or the Host, and the explanation of less common symbols is available to anyone who wishes to know it.

Many data thus seem to corroborate the cryptological view according to which the interpretation of the symbol is the object of a special knowledge, sometimes easily acces-sible, sometimes reserved to experts or to initiates, some-times forgotten today but having persisted throughout the past. This view, however, poses a particular problem – what about symbols that are not explained? And it evades a general problem – does the commentary paired to the symbol really constitute its interpretation?

Even in those societies which abundantly annotate their symbolism, it nevertheless falls short of a full coverage. Take, for example, the '*code de politesse*' in France. It is the object of numerous commentaries, inflicted on each of us from infancy, elaborated upon in manuals and treatises. Few symbolic forms are explicated to this degree. Still, even here, all the forms are not equally elaborated upon. There are some, like the handshake, which have their 'myth of origin' (one shows that one is not armed; by extending the right hand, one makes it impossible to hit the other); their 'translation' (expression of goodwill); their explicit rules of use (the initiative is to the elder, to the superior, to the woman). Or again, the fact of placing the knife and fork parallel means that one has finished eating, because it contrasts with the open position maintained during the meal. Or again, in company, yawning impolitely signifies boredom because it is a natural symptom of lassitude. In these first three cases, we have the translation of a symbol and the motivation of the translation.

Other acts, highly varied, are presented as polite or impolite, but without further elaboration: it is polite to stand up when a woman enters the room, to hold one's knife in the right hand, to cover one's mouth when yawning; impolite to point at someone, to keep one hand under the table, to pick one's nose in public. But what exactly do these different actions represent? The commentary is hesitant when one solicits it. Must we therefore say that these actions mean politeness and respect or their opposites? Just as well to say that symbols, when they are not otherwise explained, mean 'the custom' thanks to which one evades explaining them.

Finally, there are a large number of rules of politeness which are applied but never taught or explained (except, of course, at the request of the ethnographer, and then following the inspiration of the moment). Thus there is the slap on the back or the friendly tap (which are appropriate in circumstances which are intuitively precise but difficult to describe). Then there is the rule that says one must never completely empty one's glass during a meal (doubtless so as not to embarrass the host who is supposed to refill the glasses before they are completely empty). And there is the fact that when finished eating one puts the knife and fork together parallel towards the right rather than towards the left.

In other words, there is a range of symbolic behaviour concerning which the natives have fairly systematic intuitions which normally remain tacit and which it is difficult to make explicit. This symbolism works very well without any ancestor ever having had the key; there are many such examples.

Further, as we have seen, many societies have a symbolism but not a known key to it. Among those that have a key, many reserve it to a minority while the majority are witnesses of and even actors in the symbolic activity. In those societies which have a key and divulge it freely, many symbols are explained neither by that key nor by any other. If the cryptological view of symbolism were valid, it would have to admit that the mass of humanity obsessively manipulates tools whose usage it does not know, and reiterates messages whose sense it is ignorant of. As a character in Borgès says: 'It's possible, but not interesting. You will reply that reality hasn't the slightest need to be of interest. And I'll answer you that reality may avoid the obligation to be interesting, but that hypotheses may not . . .' (Borgès 1962: 130).

The hypothesis according to which the majority of symbols would be dead, or still-born – that is to say, would have lost their explanation or would never have had one – should be considered only when all others have been rejected. But this is far from being the case. We could then imagine that the exegetical commentary is one form of interpretation among others, and that – for the native as for the anthropologist – if an exegesis is lacking the other forms take precedence. Thus Turner brings together the use of symbols and their exegesis. This bringing together is appropriate; but it is far from showing that the use interprets in the manner of exegesis. It suggests, on the contrary, that the exegesis should be interpreted just as the use is. We could on the other hand imagine that proper symbolic interpretation does not depend on the exegetical commentary – so often absent – but on an unconscious, universally shared knowledge. This is Freud's (and Jones') thesis, based on significant observations, but which confuses an association which has to be interpreted with a translation which would yield the key to the symbols.

The exegetical commentary of a symbol usually includes two parts: a translation of the symbol and an optional motivation of that translation. For example, among the Ndembu, the tree *museng'u* has as its symbolic translation 'multiplicity of kills in the hunt' and this translation is motivated by the etymology of the name of the tree and by the number of fruits which it bears.

The motivation of symbols is traditionally taken as the criterion which contrasts them to signs, which are considered to be non-motivated. On closer inspection, this criterion is not very clear: firstly, for a great number of symbols no motivation is given. Secondly, etymology may constitute a sufficient symbolic motivation; linguistic signs always possess one, and often several, etymologies and would thus be sufficiently motivated to constitute symbols. Therefore the criterion, far from distinguishing signs from symbols, seems to oppose all words and some symbols on the one hand, to non-motivated symbols on the other.

In ordinary speech, this etymological motivation does not intervene and does not affect the interpretation; but it is available and one need only make it play a role for the utterance to take on symbolic value. It is therefore not symbols that must be defined as motivated, but rather a certain form of motivation that must be considered as symbolic (on motivation, etymology and symbolism, see Todorov 1972: 275–7, 282–3, 286–92).

In a semiological system, motivations must be distinguished absolutely from interpretations. The interpretations are part of the code, while the motivations are about the code and thus external to it. For example, in the lexicon the word 'roar' receives a definition 'to emit the cry characteristic of the lion'. This definition enables us to understand certain properties of the following sentences:

(1) The lion roared.
(2) The lion emitted its characteristic cry.
(3) The lion roared without making a sound.
(4) The lion roared solidly.

From the definition of 'roar' and general semantic rules, it follows that (1) and (2) are paraphrases of each other, (3) is an analytic contradiction and (4) is a semantic anomaly.

'Roar' belongs to a group of words whose semantic interpretation is partially motivated by a resemblance between their phonetic expression and the acoustic phenomena they designate – words like 'roar', 'ululate', 'miaow', 'cheep' etc. But this motivation plays no role at all in its interpretation; it does not alter any of its properties. One can understand perfectly the meaning of the word 'roar' while being ignorant of what a roar sounds like, and conversely, recognise the cry of a lion without thereby knowing how to name it. Consider for example:

(5) The lion emitted the following sound: RRRrrr!
(6) To roar is to let out a cry which resembles 'roar'.
(7) The lion roared, going 'clac clac clac clac'.

Even if 'RRRrrr!' faithfully imitates the roar of a lion, (5) is not a paraphrase of (1) and (2). Even if (6) is true, it would not be an analytic tautology. Finally, (7) is doubtless false, but it is neither an analytic contradiction nor a semantic anomaly, thus differing from (3) and (4). The motivation of 'roar' thus does not entail any particular semantic property. It is conceivable that this sort of motivation facilitates learning of vocabulary (just as do etymological motivations, learned or popular) but it plays no role in grammar.

Language does not constitute an exception in this regard; the same goes for all codes, from the very nature of the link between message and interpretation. The motivation is about the link and therefore is necessarily external to it. If the motivation were part of the interpretation of the message, it would at once cease to be a motivation, and as a motivation it could not be part of the interpretation. In other words, the motivation of a pair (message, interpretation) is not semiotic but meta-semiotic.

If we now return to the case of symbolism, and if we still take the semiological perspective there are only two possibilities: either the interpretation of the symbol consists of the translation plus the so-called motivation, that is to say, of the totality of the exegesis, and this interpretation, despite appearances, is not really motivated; or else the interpretation of the symbol is constituted by the translation alone, and the motivation is a meta-symbolic commentary. I shall now show that these two possibilities must be rejected and, with them, the particular semiological perspective that underlies them. Indeed, if symbolic motivation is not part of the interpretation, nor is it a commentary on an interpretation, the exegetical data – the only data from which the partisans of the cryptological perspective could extract the meaning of symbols and the explanation of that meaning – cannot serve this end and demand another sort of approach.

In form, symbolic motivations resemble technical ones. Just as we say that a product is good for a certain purpose because it has certain qualities, so we seem to say that an object is good for symbolising this or that because it has these or those properties.

But what characterises a technical motivation, and all rational motivation come to that, is that it is based on a general principle: if one says that glass is good for making bottles because it is transparent and tasteless, one implies that these qualities are desirable for a bottle. If one made a complete list of the desired qualities, of all products having these qualities, one could say that they are good for making bottles, and of a product having none of these qualities, that it absolutely would not suit. A motivation is only valid if it is generalisable in this way.

Symbolic motivations, on the contrary, are absolutely not generalisable. Lévi-Strauss, who devotes a chapter to this problem in *The Savage Mind*, entitled 'The Logic of Totemic Classifications', cites in particular two extravagant examples borrowed from the work of La Flesche on the Osage Indians. For them, the eagle is associated 'with lightning, lightning with fire, fire with coal and coal with the earth. The eagle is thus one of the "masters of coal" that is, a land animal' (Lévi-Strauss 1966: 59). On the other hand, the chest of the turtle with a serrated tail represents the vault of the sky, and the gray line across it, the Milky Way, because 'the number 13 has a mystical value for the Osage. The rising sun emits thirteen rays, which are divided into a group of six and a group of seven corresponding respectively to right and left, land and sky, summer and winter. The tail of this species of turtle is said to have sometimes six and sometimes seven serratures' (Lévi-Strauss 1966: 59). It was simple, but one had to be Osage to think of it.

It is possible however that an Osage who accepts these motivations without difficulty would find completely absurd the historical reasonings which seem sufficient to us to motivate the symbolism of the Union Jack or of the Cross. The Dorze would find absurd the etymological reasonings of which the Ndembu are fond. The only time I heard etymology spoken of in Dorze, it was about a statement, made by a prophet of a neighbouring society, that one should use a plant called *gesho* for a purification ritual also called *gesho*. This suggestion was cited to me as a perfect example of intellectual indigence. But though each culture discards certain types of arguments, none restricts itself to a single type.

Lévi-Strauss notes, concerning symbolic relationships, that they may be 'based on contiguity', or 'on resemblance', they may be 'sensible' or 'intelligible', 'near or far, synchronic or diachronic', 'static' or 'dynamic' (Lévi-Strauss 1966: 64–70). For these 'concrete logics', 'the existence of some connection is more important than the nature of the connections. On the formal plane, one might say they will make use of anything which comes to hand' (Lévi-Strauss 1966: 66).

This freedom of connection is particularly clear in the symbolic use of figurative language. Given any two terms, we can never exclude the possibility that one may become the symbol of the other. For example, what is it that connects the fact of leaving one's hat in the lobby and a passion for gambling? We find Balzac beginning with a metonymic relationship and going on to construct a circumstantial metaphorical relationship between these two terms. But if I take up this example it is especially because, between the first relationship and the second, Balzac ironically evokes a series of possible symbolic motivations that he does not exploit, not because they are more poorly motivated than the one which he retains, but because they do not suit his purpose:

27

'When you enter a gambling house, the law starts by stripping you of your hat.

'Is this an evangelical and providential parable?...

'Do they wish, by chance, to make it easier for you to have the pleasure of tearing your hair when you are losing?...

'Isn't it more a way of signing an infernal contract with you, by demanding I don't know what pledge?...

'Could it be to force you to maintain a respectful demeanour before those who will win your money?

'On the part of the management, there is complete silence on this point.

'But scarcely have you taken a step towards the tables, than your hat no longer belongs to you, just as you no longer belong to yourself.'

Balzac's irony is even more remarkable in that this passage opens the work, *La Peau de Chagrin*, a novel based on a metaphor and crammed with figures of speech in every sentence. It seems to show in advance that the motivation of symbols is arbitrary; after the fact, any pairing at all may be motivated, but none may be predicted.

In this area, all conceivable relations may come into play, but none is generalisable. Thus, the Cross is the symbol of the Christian religion because Christ died on a cross. By generalising the motivation, one might make the Cross the symbol of crime, because so many criminals also died on it. Or equally, one could make the nail the symbol of the Christian religion, because Christ died pierced by nails. But in the first instance, the motivation that works for the gallows, the guillotine or the electric chair does not work for the cross. In the second instance, the motivation that works not only for the cross but also for the shroud, and the crown of thorns, need not work for the nail. Neither these extensions nor these exclusions may be predicted, and if they seem 'natural' it is only after the fact. Symbolic motivations only have the appearance of motivations, and in their case rather than of logic, it is of paralogism that we must speak.

This same lack of generalisability that makes motivations fail as discourse *on* symbolism conversely characterises them as a discourse *in* symbolism, and not at all as a discourse that interprets but, on the contrary, as a discourse that must be interpreted.

The motivation of the translation of a symbol is only one case among others of symbolic motivation. It can be compared to the motivation of the ritual use of an object, to which it is sometimes joined. The Ndembu first explain that the *museng'u* is good for a certain hunting ritual because it means 'a multiplicity of kills'; secondly, that it means this by the etymology of its name and the abundance of its fruits. These are the two stages of a single reasoning. Moreover, is the intermediate reference to meaning really necessary? When the Ndembu wish to mean 'a multiplicity of kills' they simply use the words of their language and not a branch of *museng'u*. They use the latter when they wish, not to mean, but to obtain 'game in abundance'. And even supposing that the Ndembu expressly say that the *museng'u* 'means' multiplicity (but Turner never makes clear what Ndembu concept he translates by 'meaning'), it would be no less the case that the tree is utilised *because* it means, and not *to* mean 'multiplicity'.

The exegetical motivation of *museng'u* poses the same problem as the ritual use of the *museng'u*: they are both based on a principle that is not generalisable – the one does not explain the meaning, the other does not explain the ritual. For the Ndembu, the two explanations are, undoubtedly, both valid. But this consideration shifts the problem and does not solve it. For like all other human beings, the Ndembu as soon as they reason, know tacitly that the validity of an argument depends on the general principle that underlies it, unless the argument is not logically, but symbolically, interpreted.

The symbolic character of a motivation is not due to the fact that it applies to a symbol, it is rather the object that becomes symbolic by virtue of the motivation that is applied to it. This is the case for words once one links their meaning to a superfluous motivation.

Compare the two utterances:

(8) The lion roared.

(9) The lion RRrroared.

(8) is pronounced normally while in (9), the initial 'r' is heavily rolled. The semantic interpretation of these two utterances is the same: they admit the same paraphrases, they can be contradicted in the same way, they have the same truth value. But (9) necessarily receives, over and above that semantic interpretation that it shares with (8), a symbolic interpretation that is its own; and that because the rolling of the 'r' evokes the motivation of 'roar'.

Following the same principle, current advertising practice transforms utilitarian objects into symbols by giving to their use non-generalisable motivations. For example:

'Take the time to try it on. Get into a Noblet suit... and hear once again the real story of the world's most beautiful cloth. Noblet cloth is cloth that has something to say.'

As in the case of the *museng'u*, use Noblet cloth *because* it means something! Or again:

'This lighter has the strength of today's man. The one who decides and succeeds. For its Mach 2, Braun has rejected prettiness. It is sober. Functional. Black. Like a weapon. With the Braun Mach 2, the future is in our pockets. Are you ready?'

In this context, even the valid argument ('functional') is used symbolically. As for the name 'Mach 2', it is used not to mean, but once again because it means 'twice the speed of sound', a notion which has nothing to do with the use of a lighter.

If motivation has a symbolic effect in so far as it does not motivate (and the sign to the extent that it does not just mean something) we may understand, then, that intentional non-motivation can play the same role. In an advertisement for Akaï tape recorders, the argument is drawn from the fact that:

'No one has yet been able to explain why the ferrite crystal alone eliminates the background noise which is normally found on all magnetic tape.'

Like pseudo-motivations, non-motivations establish the truth of a statement not by demonstrating it, but by presupposing it. Similarly, a Dorze would find confirmation of his beliefs in:

'No one knows any more how to explain why only the *oloma* eliminates ritual taboos that are normally encountered on private land.'

Thus, the refusal of exegesis, just as exegesis itself, may be the object of a symbolic interpretation, for both contrast, though in different ways, with real motivation. If a child asks its mother why it is not allowed to put its finger in its nose, and if she answers either 'Because it is not done', or else 'Because one day a little boy put his finger in his nose and couldn't get it out again', the child knows perfectly well that nothing has been motivated. 'Because it is not done' is a refusal of exegesis. Exegesis in the form of a tale is not generalisable: if the child demonstrated that he himself was safe from such an accident, the prohibition would be maintained nonetheless. In the two cases, the task of interpretation remains entire. In the second, it concerns not only the prohibition, but its motivation as well.

Now imagine that an Ndembu who asks the 'why' of the *museng'u* meets with the reply, 'It is the custom', instead of with an exegesis. The fact that the *museng'u* enters into gynecological ritual on the one hand, and into hunting ritual on the other, already orients the possible interpretations by suggesting a relationship between these two rituals. For example in the two cases it is a question of obtaining in large number that which is lacking – children or game. It is a question further of making visible that which is hidden – children in the womb, game in the bush.

The relating may be done not only by a parallel, but also by a contrast; in one case it is a matter of giving life to humans, in the other, of taking it from animals. Actually, the use of the *museng'u* also sets up a contrast between the two types of ritual. In gynecological rituals, it is the bark of the *museng'u* which, together with that of other species, is crushed to make a potion with which the beneficiary of the ritual is aspersed. In hunting rituals, it is a branch stripped of its bark and whittled into a point that is planted alone, and without being allowed to fall on the ground, to be aspersed by the beneficiary of the ritual. A contrast, therefore, between a container and a content, between a mixture and a clearly isolated object, between a crushing and an erecting, between a moistening preparation and a moistened object.

All these data, these parallels, these contrasts, constitute indices by means of which experience may be organized, indices which suggest certain themes and discard others. Exegesis brings other indices to bear. Thus, in this case, it corroborates the theme of multiplicity, sets aside the theme of visibility (reserved for another tree; cf. Turner 1967: 288–9) and remains mute on the contrast between the two uses of the *museng'u*. Turner therefore has reason to relate the use of symbols and their exegesis, for both limit and orient the field of possible interpretations. But then, nothing justifies the making of this link under the general heading of meaning for, as Turner himself shows clearly, neither usage nor exegesis defines or constitutes a closed set of possible inter-pretations, a set of given pairs (symbol, interpretation). Moreover, to take the view suggested here is merely to follow the metaphorical expression that the Ndembu use to designate symbols: the word *chijikijilu*, which means 'a landmark'. A landmark is not a sign but an index which serves cognitively to organise our experience of space. This Ndembu metaphor seems much more apposite and subtle to me than the Western metaphor which compares symbols to words.

As may be seen, I disagree with Turner only on a single point: the use he makes of the notion of meaning – in his eyes a descriptive category, in mine a misleading metaphor. If I have used his works, it is not to underscore this disagreement, but on the contrary because his analyses implicitly discard the idea of a symbolism organised like a code, so that he cannot speak of meaning except by refraining from defining or even circumscribing the concept. It would be better, in fact, not to speak of meaning at all, since talk of meaning offers only one, rather suspect advantage: it prevents us from asking, 'If not meaning, what?' I shall return to this later.

To summarise, we have examined four types of data:
– Symbols of which no translation is given (for example, the *oloma*).
– Symbols of which a translation is given, but which are not used to mean that translation; rather, it is the translation that is used to motivate the symbol. Similarly, when this translation is itself motivated, that second motivation is only a development of the motivation of the symbol (for example, the *museng'u*).
– Technical objects which become symbolic through their motivation (for example, the Mach 2 lighter).
– Signs which become symbolic not to the extent that they mean something, but to the extent that that meaning is motivated (for example, 'roar').

It emerges from this examination: firstly, that the motivation of symbols (of which exegesis is a particular case) is not meta-symbolic but symbolic. Secondly, that this motivation is not an interpretation of symbols but, on the contrary, must itself be interpreted symbolically. The two potentially useful paths for a cryptological view of symbolism to follow (motivation is meta-symbolic, or else motivation is part of the interpretation) are therefore both closed. The data on which this conception rests, far from yielding the meaning of symbols, remain, on the contrary, open to interpretation.

No conscious and shared knowledge justifies a semiological view of symbolism. I have shown that the unshared conscious knowledge, which constitutes the exegesis of symbols, also fails in this respect; exegesis is not an interpretation but rather an extension of the symbol and must itself be interpreted. A final hypothesis remains possible: the second term of the pairs (symbol, interpretation) necessary to a semiological approach might be part of an unconscious knowledge; symbols might be interpreted according to a code that humans share, without being aware of it.

Such a view was explicitly stated by Sigmund Freud in the tenth of his *Introductory Lectures on Psycho-Analysis* (Freud 1963) in which he takes up and develops his sparse remarks in *The Interpretation of Dreams*. Freud here contrasts the ordinary elements of dreams for which 'we never obtain constant translations' with symbols for which 'we obtain constant translations... just as popular "dream-books" provide them for *everything* that appears in dreams' (Freud 1963: 150). He defines 'a constant relation of this kind between a dream-element and its translation . . . as a "symbolic" one, and the dream-element itself as a "symbol" of the unconscious dream-thought' (Freud 1963: 150). Further, 'these symbolic relations are not something peculiar to dreamers or to the dream-work through which they come to expression. This same symbolism, as we have seen, is employed by myths and fairy tales, by the people in their sayings and songs, by colloquial linguistic usage and by the poetic imagination. The field of symbolism is immensely wide, and dream-symbolism is only a small part of it' (Freud 1963: 166).

Whatever the extension Freud attributes to symbolism, his definition of it is less comprehensive than in current usage. Many psychoanalysts have not followed him on this point. To cite only one of them, Guy Rosolato writes that: 'the plurivalence implied by the symbol is opposed to the conventional univalence of certain relationships of the signifier and the signified' (1969: 113); to define the symbol, he cites a passage from *The Interpretation of Dreams* where it is the ordinary elements of the dream that are defined and precisely *not* the symbols which Freud contrasts with them. We may accept, indeed, that Freud's contribution to a theory of symbolism goes far beyond the few pages that he devotes directly to it, and is essentially located elsewhere.

I do not intend to examine this general contribution. If we extend the notion of symbolism to include the ordinary elements of the dream which, according to Freud himself, do not form stable pairs with their interpretations, we exclude, by the same token, the symbolism from the semiological field as I have defined it. Conversely, symbolism in the restricted sense conceived by Freud enters very clearly into that field. If I discuss that view, it is therefore neither to evaluate nor even to place the work of Freud from the point of view of a general theory of symbolism; rather it is only because it provides an exemplary instance of the semiological view of symbolism as an unconscious code.

Freud restricts the notion of symbolism to dream or cultural elements systematically paired with unconscious representations. We are thus confronted with two problems: on the one hand, that of establishing the existence of these pairs and of describing them; on the other, that of deciding whether

35

it is really a question of (messages, interpretation) pairs form-ing a code, thus justifying a semiological view of symbolism.

The existence of pairs (symbol, unconscious representa-tion) is by nature hypothetical, but that is not where the problem lies. If such an hypothesis permits us to account for otherwise incomprehensible or poorly-understood data, it surely merits being retained. For example, certain Dorze dignitaries called *halak'a*, during rituals attendant on their entry into office, adorn their foreheads with brass objects which represent, in fairly realistic manner, an erect penis. When I stressed this resemblance to my informants, after having waited in vain for them to mention it to me spon-taneously, my remark was taken as a joke in bad taste. Two possibilities then: either the resemblance is fortuitous – yet how well chance arranges things! – or else the resemblance plays a role unconsciously. Even the ethnographer who is most hostile to psychoanalysis is tempted to baptise as 'phallic' symbols which his informants describe in a com-pletely different way.

Such interpretations are still far from the Freudian view; they presuppose the possibility of unconscious relationships and nothing more. They do not however presuppose that these unconscious representations, though related to sym-bols, must regularly be paired with them. The logic of these ordinary relationships is the same, be they accomplished consciously or unconsciously; they may make themselves obvious or scarcely be motivated; they may be felt by several or by one alone; they may enlighten or confound; they have no privileged domain.

Conversely, the relationships Freud speaks of are typically unconscious, inevitable, universal and limited in range. Symbols, in his scheme of things, represent the human body, parents, children, brothers, sisters, birth, death, nakedness, and above all, the area of sexual life, the genitals and sexual processes and intercourse (Freud 1963).

The systematic pairing of such representations with symbols does not pose too many problems. A large number of symbolic objects are already masculine or feminine. If we examine form and movement, from down to up, from before to behind, from inside to outside, and vice versa, a dry or humid, hard or soft character, everything works out fine . . . and better still since in case of doubt the theory excludes neither ambiguous symbols that admit of two interpretations at once, nor unexpected symbols whose meaning is indirectly established. The underlying logic is that of a trivial party game: 'If it were a sexual phenomenon, what would it be?'

An example: during certain rituals, the Dorze place a piece of butter on their heads. Many connections are possible, of which some are clearly made by the Dorze themselves, but the rules of the game are to keep to the question: If this butter were a sexual phenomenon. . .? Undoubtedly, semen. And why put it on one's head? Because the head and especially the hair symbolise the genitals (see, for example, Berg 1951, discussed by Leach [1958]).

The intrigued ethnographer tries to corroborate this hypothesis and finds that relevant data are not lacking. Butter is consumed melted, in a liquid form, and preserved in oval pats (like testicles) wrapped in leaves, and often attached two or three together. The dignitaries whose foreheads are adorned with a penis must keep a piece of butter on their heads during their entire term in office. They must not cut their hair. They must be married. They ensure the fertility of humans and of cattle. Their wives during the same period also have their heads buttered and, moreover, keep their hair in the shape of a raised diadem in which the pubis might be recognisable. Even more spectacular, butter enters into marriage ceremonies, young men wear a piece on their heads, but above all, the hairdo of young married women is twice covered by a veritable skullcap of butter.

In all these cases, butter is placed on the heads of persons who thenceforward will be fertile, or who are guarantors of fertility; and thus, the hypothesis of its symbolic association with semen seems to receive initial confirmation. But in order to preserve this hypothesis, it is necessary not so much to find a certain number of facts that are compatible with it – which is easy and proves nothing – but above all to show that it has explanatory and predictive value. We would need to show, for example, that the ritual affirmation of fertility, and the ritual use of butter, are regularly paired; a relationship between butter and fertility, in itself obscure enough, in effect becomes clear if butter is a symbolic equivalent of semen. If the hypothesis is not restricted in this way, it is more attractive than useful. Yet, if one restricts it in these terms, many data then seem to go against it.

The dignitaries of whom I spoke are not the only guarantors of fertility. More clearly than they, the big sacrificers (*demutsa*) play the same role. Like them, they must be married; they never cut their hair; they observe several similar prohibitions. But they do not wear butter on their heads. Further, there are many sacrifices carried out by the elders of the lineage segment, of the lineage or the clan whose expressed aim is to guarantee the fertility of the group, in which butter does not come into play at all. Therefore, fertility can go equally well without butter.

Conversely, if a man has killed either an enemy in war, or a wild animal such as a lion, a leopard or an elephant, he must carry out a special ritual with the customary bit of butter on his head. Such an exploit is not supposed to lead to an increase in fertility; it merely assures its author a new status and increased prestige, marked by songs, emblems, and later by funerary rites above the ordinary. Therefore butter may also go without fertility.

If butter is not systematically associated with fertility, it is still, in an absolute manner, associated with changes in status. All rites of passage (from bachelorhood to marriage, from ordinary status to that of dignitary, from that of ordinary man to that of killer, etc.) are doubly marked by the use of butter and by a ceremonial circumambulation of the market place. Succession to the title of big sacrificer goes from father to eldest son, and is not marked by any ritual; in the mind of the Dorze there is in this instance a continuity without transition and thus without butter. On the other hand, dignitaries are chosen, and not only their installation, but the whole duration of their incumbency in office is a passage between the status of ordinary man and that of 'father of the country'; a passage marked by a daily use of butter.

Once butter is associated with transition and not with fertility, its symbolic identification with semen, far from explaining anything, raises a further problem. The ethnographer then resorts to a more classic solution: butter is, for the Dorze, the rich food *par excellence*, the symbol of prestige as regards food; and its ritual use is a typical case of conspicuous consumption. Other forms of conspicuous consumption are linked, among the Dorze, to rites of passage; but no food, no artifact, lends itself so well as butter. Unlike drinks, it is visible (it is spiced butter which melts very slowly and which, put on in the morning, is still there in the evening). It is available the whole year round in as small quantities as desired, unlike meat which means slaughtering an animal and which does not preserve well. It stays on the head better than other foods. It is evidence of a renewed expenditure, unlike made objects which last too long, etc. In short, it is the perfect marker of an ostentatious expenditure, associated not with rituals which are particularly sexual, but with all rites of passage and with them alone. An extraordinary expenditure is contrasted to parsimony as the transition is contrasted to permanent statuses: therein lies a quasi-universal symbolism. Think, for example, of baptismal, marriage or communion feasts in our society with their rich foods, their special clothes, their gifts, often made of precious metals.

The hypothesis of a sexual symbolism and, more especially, of an unconscious representation of semen by means of butter, is not weakened for all that. It is enough to modify it as follows: rites of passage alone are associated with an ostentatious expenditure of butter, but this expenditure itself represents a seminal expenditure all the more meaningful in that in Dorze eroticism, the accent is placed on seminal retention.

As foreseen by Freudian theory, a similar opposition re-emerges at a 'pre-genital' level. Colic is considered the signal symptom of digestive troubles, while a state of relative constipation is considered normal. However, the Dorze use a powerful laxative of vegetable origin not only as a remedy for all stomach complaints, but even from time to time without any circumstantial reason; for its regular use is considered beneficial and purifying. The weakness induced by colic is noted and even exaggerated. Thus, in a story recorded by Luc Desmarquest (1970) an invincible hero is finally captured by his adversaries when he is under the effect of a laxative. One could compare this to the state of weakness attributed to young married women when they have their heads covered with butter – old women support them as though they were in danger of swooning at any moment. Further, if fecal activity does not enter into rites of passage, urine does have its place. Right in the middle of the ceremonial tour of the market place which marks these rituals, the men stop and urinate in a line. Yet another ostentatious expenditure which contrasts with an habitual discretion.

There is, therefore, in the Dorze ideology, a marked contrast between retention and expenditure, between parsimony and prodigality, the one governing daily life and guaranteeing security; the other ritually necessary but dangerous all the same. This contrast, very explicit in the realm of economics, extends implicitly but clearly to other realms and in particular to organic life. Within this general contrast, a relationship between the ritual expenditure of butter, expenditure of semen and of faeces is certainly possible, if not inevitable. The problem now is whether this relationship really defines a pair (symbol, interpretation).

I shall show that the relationship of butter to semen in this context is neither necessary nor sufficient for the interpretation, and that it therefore does not define a semiological pair. First of all, imagine a Dorze to whom the relationship in question would be neither implicitly nor unconsciously apparent. For all that, he would not be brought up short. This butter on the head would give him ample food for thought. For the Dorze, economic expenditure has a more definite daily relevance than does seminal expenditure, and butter represents the first synecdochically, as well as the second metaphorically. The fact that certain rituals are marked by butter connects them and isolates an implicit category of rites of passage. The transitional character of the office of dignitary is thus marked by opposition to that of sacrificer. Many other associations are possible, but it is enough to show that the symbolic use of butter contributes to giving Dorze ritual life its cognitive organisation, independent of all exegesis and of all Freudian unconscious.

Suppose now that a Freudian unconscious enters in and associates butter with semen. There is no reason to think that the other associations thereby lose their relevance. In certain theories of symbolism one interpretation chases out another; in reality there is always room for new associations. The association with semen links Dorze ritual life (already linked to economic life) with organic life, and enriches the symbolic value of butter, while not by itself defining it.

Ernest Jones, in his essay 'The Theory of Symbolism' in

which he defends and develops Freud's position, brings up
the problem posed by the multiplicity of symbolic associations. As he points out, these associations are much more
numerous and diverse than those proposed by Freud. The
latter may even all be missing without this making interpretation impossible. The systematic pairing of several thousand symbols with a hundred or so ideas – says Jones –
seems again brought into question. Nevertheless, Jones
justifies it by two considerations. Firstly, only unconscious
associations are really symbolic: 'Only what is repressed is
symbolised; only what is repressed needs to be symbolised.
This conclusion is the touchstone of the psycho-analytic
theory of symbolism' (Jones 1967: 116). Secondly, 'the pri-
mary ideas of life [are] the only ones that can be symbolised
– those namely concerning the bodily self, the relation to
the family, birth, love, and death' (Jones 1967: 116). In
other words, he asserts that two criteria – unconscious
character on the one hand, and belonging to a short list
of possible symbolisations on the other – are co-extensive,
and that therefore the data isolated by Freud do constitute
an autonomous system.

Other associations of symbols are conscious or may become
conscious (explicit or implicit but not unconscious) and are
not *symbolic* but *metaphorical*. 'It is very common indeed
to find a combination in this respect, so that the figure in
question is partly symbolical – that is, it represents unconscious mental attitudes and ideas – and partly metaphorical –
that is, it indicates other collateral ideas. In some uses the
symbolical meaning may be entirely absent' as in the case
of a Dorze who would not even unconsciously associate
butter with semen. There is then 'the replacement of symbolism by metaphor'. If a Dorze makes that association
among others, we would say that 'the symbolical meaning
is present at the same time as the metaphorical' (Jones
1967: 126).

I grant that the conscious or unconscious nature of an association has considerable importance. There is, nevertheless, some arbitrariness in making it 'the touchstone' of symbolism. In so doing, one eliminates, as the cryptological view does not, all the exegesis because one does not see more than metaphorical developments in it. But this is not the principal objection to Jones' view. It is easy enough to show that the two criteria he retains – the unconscious nature of the symbolised and its belonging to a narrow and specific domain – are not co-extensive; that the boundary that separates the symbolic from the metaphorical in Jones' terms is mobile and permeable and does not isolate a definite set of possible symbolisations. Consequently, the postulated systematic pairing collapses.

Ethnographers have reported a considerable number of cases of perfectly conscious sexual symbolism, data which the partisans of the Freudian view of symbolism treat by supposing that 'primitives' are less repressed than we. In this regard, Leach (1958) criticised Charles Berg's book (1951) on the symbolism of hair: 'an essential part of Berg's argument [is that] in civilized society, the libidinal nature of hair rituals must be unconscious, although for reasons which are not clear to me, he is prepared to grant greater insight to the unsophisticated Australian aborigines... This kind of argument involves a distinction between civilized and non-civilized societies which most anthropologists find difficult to accept or even to understand. Is it really the case that the weight of modern civilisation always pushes the significance of sexual symbols deep into the "unconscious"? And if so, just where does modern civilisation begin?' (Leach 1958: 154). Leach gives several examples of perfectly conscious sexual interpretation of symbols linked with hair, taken from Indian and Ceylonese societies which, if one accepts the concept, are certainly 'civilized'. In the same line of argument, one could ask oneself not only where modern civilisation begins, but also where it ends. For the popularisation of Freud's work has led to the considerable development of a conscious sexual symbolism. Is this to say, in Jones' terms, that we are no longer dealing with symbolism but rather with metaphor? Or is it to say that we are now symbolising like 'primitives' again, and not like the 'civilised'? These are conclusions which would be unacceptable even to psychoanalysts.

Among the Dorze themselves, the boundary between the explicit and the tacit is often easier to trace than that between the conscious and the unconscious. My informants do not deny that the brass object placed on the heads of dignitaries resembles an erect penis; they deny only that this commentary – like all commentaries on symbols – is relevant; implicit knowledge, therefore, but not unconscious. If one does not explicitly wear a penis on one's head, it is however quite overtly that one hangs the penises of one's enemies – killed and emasculated – on the wall not far from the chairs in which one is accustomed to sit. The two social statuses linked to these rituals – that of dignitary and that of killer – are explicitly related. Here one has the principle of an association which is definitely tacit, but not necessarily unconscious.

The association between the ritual use of butter and the idea of a deliberate and ostentatious expenditure, one desired for its own sake, seems more probably unconscious to me. Certainly, the Dorze repeat that butter is costly. But the idea that tradition imposes its use upon them not *despite* but in fact *because of* its costliness would scandalize them. Similarly, tradition obliges new dignitaries literally to ruin themselves through public feasting. But that the economic weakening that results from this is not a bitterly resented side inconvenience but rather an essential and symbolically necessary aspect of these rituals, would be a profoundly shocking view to a people who make parsimony a virtue. The expenditure is thus perfectly explicit, but its symbolic value is probably unconscious.

The comparison between the economic weakening that results from this expenditure and the physiological weakening caused by ejaculation or purges is certainly tacit, but much less incapable of becoming conscious. In the Dorze system of taboos, economic weakness and physiological weakness arise from the same etiology. There are weakenings which are endured by the living who follow the tradition of the dead – in the case of ritual, ejaculation, and purge; and there are those provoked by the dead to counter the living who have disobeyed the traditions – in the case of taboos. As Dorze theory explicitly deals with all the weakenings due to taboos in the same way, it is not absurd to imagine an implicit treatment common to all weakenings due to rituals.

In short, if one examines a concrete symbolic system in its entirety, instead of remaining content to assemble isolated examples found here and there that conform to the thesis one wishes to defend, it seems clear that symbolic associations are multiplex, that they may be culturally explicit or implicit, individually conscious or unconscious, inside or outside the domain of interpretations defined by Freud (and after him by Jones) without these three distinctions overlapping. In these conditions, the problem posed by this multiplicity of symbolic associations remains entire, and Jones' attempt to resolve it fails. The proposed distinction between the symbolic and the metaphorical is based on two criteria that are not co-extensive, and therefore it must be abandoned. The associations proposed by Freud may enter into symbolic interpretation but they are not necessary to it.

It will now be simple to show that in any case, these associations are not sufficient either, and that even if we supposed that they were always made, and made exclusively (which Jones said clearly was not the case) they do not constitute an interpretation of symbols. Considered as interpretations, these associations are not, in fact, less mysterious than the symbols themselves. Suppose that the ethnographer, having translated 'butter on the head' by 'semen on the genitals' takes to his heels and says, 'I have understood'. What exactly has he understood? What makes the fact of symbolically putting semen on one's genitals during certain public rituals more comprehensible than the fact of actually putting butter on one's head? The problem of interpretation is modified – as in the case of any association – but it is in no way resolved.

In order to interpret a symbol with an associated idea one should not substitute the second term of the association for the first, but rather consider them together. I shall take an example from Freud: a pistol may be a symbol of the penis. But if it is particularly appropriate, it is as much because of their differences as because of their similarities. The pistol, as against the penis, is an instrument detached from the body, always rigid, always rechargeable, capable of working at a distance, by means of solid emissions. The symbolic relationship between the pistol and the penis is therefore one of contrast as much as resemblance, of opposition as much as representation, and it therefore is not a question of interpreting the symbol 'pistol' by means of the translation 'penis' but of interpreting the association pistol–penis which is an interpretation in appearance only.

There are other ways than Freud's of conceiving of symbolism as an unconscious code. If I have chosen to discuss his rather than another, it is because it is particularly clear and explicit and because Freud never modified it (nor developed it, for that matter). Jung's view is richer and more complex though he never gave it a clear and compact formulation to which he might have held. It is customary in France to criticise Jung without having studied his work, and to accentuate his weaknesses while ignoring his original contributions. Conversely, we pass lightly over Freud's weaknesses – for example, his theory of symbolism is often ignored by those who claim to follow him. This is at once too much and too little respect. Freud at least had the merit of giving a precise scope to his view and envisaged symbolism as a code in which each symbol would find its prefigured interpretation. The arguments put forward here weigh not against one or another detail of that conception, nor against the particular observations whose formulation it permits, but rather against its very premise; and they would weigh equally against any view that posited a set of pairs (symbol, unconscious interpretation), that is to say, against any semiological view of symbolism as an unconscious code.

It will have been noted that the two semiological views discussed – the cryptological and the Freudian – fail because of two inverse and two parallel defects. The inverse defects derive from a considerable disproportion between symbols and the representations they are said to encode. In one case, a restricted number of explicit symbols is associated with certain representations in such an unruly manner that any object at all could as well have been symbolised. An arbitrary exegesis makes an unforeseeable selection among all these possible symbolisations. In the other case, a restricted number of unconscious representations may be encoded by any object at all, real or imaginary, which becomes a symbol by the same token. The cryptological view posits at the outset a set of symbols as given in a culture; the Freudian view posits at the outset a set of interpretations as given in the unconscious. Both leave the logic of the relationships (symbol, interpretation) largely indeterminate or even posit this indeterminateness as an intrinsic characteristic of symbolism.

In the next chapter, we shall study the structuralist view which, on the contrary, posits a logic of relationships at the outset, but leaves its terms indeterminate – a more acceptable view but, paradoxically, not a semiological one at all.

The parallel defects of the cryptological and Freudian views derive from a poor appreciation of the nature of the pairs (symbol, exegesis) and (symbol, representation). In both cases, and contrary to predictions, the second terms of the pairs are not substituted for, but rather are added to, the first. Exegesis, like unconscious representation, does not constitute the interpretation of the symbol, but one of its extensions, and must itself be symbolically interpreted.

If we recognise that in these pairs, the second term is not an interpretation but a development of the first, we can as well consider that the first is a development of the second – that the idea of the pistol is a development of the idea of the penis; the *museng'u* a development of the idea of multiplicity; the ritual use of butter a development of conspicuous consumption. Symbolic pairs are undoubtedly oriented; their terms are rarely permutable. But they are oriented along different axes, from the concrete to the abstract, from the general to the particular, from the explicit to the tacit, and one cannot deduce from the position of a term on one axis the position it will occupy on others.

Since, moreover, the semiological axis of *signifiant–signifié* or message–interpretation is absent; since symbolic elements enter not into one pairing alone but into a set of associations; since the interpretation bears not on the elements but on their configuration, it is the very notion of the symbol that must be brought into question. Todorov notes: 'The symbol is not necessarily the essential notion of symbolism, no more than the word is the essential notion of language' (Todorov 1972: 284). In my view, the criticism must be carried even further. Even if the analysis of a sentence into words is a surface fact which plays an important role only in phonological representation, as long as such an analysis may be carried out the notion of a word may be clearly enough defined. Symbolic configurations comprise a large number of elements; but which of them are the symbols? All? Some? To what definition must they conform to count as such? What theoretical import would such a definition have? Is the very notion of the symbol necessary?

The view that a symbolic phenomenon may be analysed into symbols usually arises from the semiological illusion according to which it is symbols that constitute the *signifiant*, the interpreted message. This illusion is not only an artifact of theoreticians limited to an academic audience. It often constitutes a cultural phenomenon, a conscious theory that the natives – Westerners or Ndembu for example – have of their own symbolism. This native theory acts in turn on symbolic practice itself. It defines certain manipulable elements as symbols. It fosters the exegetical development of symbolism. It favours certain forms of symbolic configurations.

But if symbolism may be influenced by this theory, it is not the product of it. This influence is not effective unless it acts within the constraints of symbolism itself. Attempts to construct a symbolic system by placing symbols end to end are generally repaid by failure: nothing could be less symbolically efficacious than the Cult of the Supreme Being founded by Robespierre, or the sexual symbols of intellectually pretentious pornographic films. These manipulations of symbols certainly provoke effects, but never quite those that were anticipated. It is not that these symbols once put into play are difficult to decode; on the contrary. It is just that the decoding of symbols is neither necessary nor sufficient to constitute a symbolical system.

The very notion of the symbol is a secondary and cultural development of the universal phenomenon that is symbolism. Such a notion is, to my knowledge, absent among the Dorze, and we have seen that it takes one form among the Ndembu, and another among ourselves. In our own culture, there is no agreement on the definition and extension of the notion of the symbol. The Cross, the Union Jack, the handshake, yawning, the word 'roar' with an accentuated rolling of the 'r', the synecdoche 'sail' for 'boat', the metaphor 'fox' for 'cunning man', the metonymy 'sleep together' for 'make love', the Rolls Royce, the Braun Mach 2 lighter, all these elements have or may take on a symbolic value. But which are symbols? And who will agree on that?

The semiological illusion aside, there is no need for an analysis of the symbolic phenomenon into symbols. The notion of a symbol is not universal but cultural, present or absent, differing from culture to culture, or even within a given culture. It is subject to the same sort of critical analysis as that formulated by Rodney Needham (1972) concerning the notion of belief. I suggest, therefore, that the notion of the symbol, at least provisionally, be removed from the vocabulary of the theory of symbolism, and be described only as a native notion.

We now see more clearly why the two semiological views discussed so far – the cryptological and the Freudian – are bound to fail. They both agree, without prior discussion, to answer the question 'What do symbols mean?' Yet this question presupposes, firstly, that symbols are defined and secondly, that they do have meaning. As these presuppositions are erroneous, the question as posed is impossible to answer. And that is exactly where its symbolic import lies: the inevitable failure of all attempts assures, at one and the same time, their reduplication. Thus, exegetical and psychoanalytical attempts seem to obey a cultural plan – in appearance, to interpret symbolism; in fact to recreate it. For all keys to symbols are part of symbolism itself.

3

Absent Meaning

Semiologists – I mean self-avowed ones – might feel that if the preceding chapters were aimed at them they have gone wide of the mark. Indeed, the cryptological and psychoanalytic conceptions were elaborated outside the semiological framework proposed by Ferdinand de Saussure:

'A language is a system of signs that express ideas, and is therefore comparable to a system of writing, to the alphabet of deaf-mutes, symbolic rites, polite formulas, military signals, etc. But it is the most important of all these systems.

'*A science that studies the life of signs within society* is conceivable; it would be a part of social psychology and consequently, of general psychology; I shall call it *semiology* (from Greek *sémeîon*, "sign"). It would show what constitutes signs, what laws govern them' (Saussure 1959: 16).

In a semiology thus conceived, the fundamental question is no longer 'What do symbols mean?' but 'How do they mean?' These two questions are clearly linked. Pre- or para-Saussurian semiologists who are concerned above all with the what-question support their analyses with hypotheses about the 'how'; conversely, the question 'how' presupposes the knowledge of 'what'. Saussurian semiology therefore does not *in principle* constitute a radical break, but rather a shift of interest within a semiological approach which existed in the West long before it was known as such. I say 'in principle' because in fact, Saussurian semiologists have completely left aside the what-question, and have studied not

51

at all 'How do symbols mean?', but rather 'How do symbols work?' In this study they have established, all unknowing, that symbols work without meaning. Modern semiology, and this is at once its weakness and its merit, has refuted the principles on which it is founded.

The study of symbolism under the heading of Saussurian semiology only developed fully after the Second World War, and especially in the works of Claude Lévi-Strauss, to which my discussion will be limited. The arguments I shall put forward may, it seems to me, be extended to other expressly semiological perspectives in so far as these are clear, which is not always the case.

Lévi-Strauss formed largely new views on symbolism which do not fall under my previous arguments. The critique of the semiological conception as I have developed it so far would therefore be unfair and paradoxical if it were not that the paradox, as I shall show, is not of my making, but that of the semiologists themselves. Unlike the views discussed above, those of the semiologists are not semiological at all; despite a terminology borrowed from linguistics, symbols are not treated as signs. The symbolic signifier, freed from the signified, is no longer a real signifier except by a dubious metaphor whose only merit is to avoid the problem of the nature of symbolism, not to resolve it.

In the cryptological and Freudian views of symbolism, an element became a symbol from the mere fact of receiving an interpretation. In the Freudian view and in some of the cryptological ones, over and above that, the interpretations belong to a single domain. Two different principles are the basis of the study of symbolism proposed by Lévi-Strauss. Firstly, an element never of itself receives a symbolic interpretation, but only in so far as it is opposed to at least one other element. Secondly, there is not one unique domain of interpretation, but a set of domains (which Lévi-Strauss calls 'codes') in which symbolic oppositions are interpreted.

The import of these principles becomes clearer if we return to the example of Dorze butter.

Butter on the head is only symbolic in so far as it is opposed to butter as ordinarily consumed. In its alimentary use, butter is consumed melted, in limited quantities, and as a sort of sauce. In its ritual use, it is solid, used in large quantities, and by itself. The opposition is thus between a modest and discreet normal usage and an expensive and ostentatious ritual usage. Similarly, meals which accompany rituals are doubly opposed to daily meals: quantity on the one hand, and quality on the other; for foods of animal origin – butter and meat – take pride of place in them.

In the economic domain, ritual is marked by a generous expenditure without a view toward profit, and daily life, by a modest expenditure and by calculated investments. In the same area, normal participation in market activities is discreet (no patter to attract customers) and respectful of others (great care is taken not to disarrange stalls); the ceremonial tour of the market, by contrast, is done by dashing aside, violently if necessary, every obstacle on a route that does not respect the normal market pathways. In the sociological domain, there is the same opposition between established statuses that are known by all and which it is generally bad form to wax expansive about, and the period that marks a change of status in which it is proper, on the contrary, to attract public notice. In the physiological domain, there is an opposition between recommended seminal retention and fertile incontinence; and opposition between 'normal' constipation and purifying purge. Further data would allow us to add further oppositions in the same domain or in others to complete the accompanying table.

	Moderation	Excess
Culinary domain	Butter on food	Butter on the head
	Food in limited quantity, especially of vegetable origin	Abundant food, especially of animal origin
Economic domain	Parsimony and search for profit	Expenditure and generosity
	Discreet and respectful market participation	Showy and brutal ritual activity in the market
Sociological domain	Modesty about established status	Ostentatious affirmation of change of status
Physiological domain	Constipation	Purge
	Seminal retention	Seminal expenditure

In such a table, the first term $X1$ of a row X is opposed to a second term $X2$, as the first term, $Y1$, of a row Y is opposed to a second term $Y2$, thus giving the canonical formula of structural analyses of symbolism:

$$X1 : X2 : : Y1 : Y2$$

which is read $X1$ is to $X2$ as $Y1$ is to $Y2$. Thus, for example, alimentary butter is to ritual butter as modesty about status is to the ostentatiousness of the rite of passage, etc. In a given ritual, or a particular text of oral tradition, only some of these oppositions are manifest, but a tacit reference to absent oppositions is made possible. The dichotomy message/interpretation (if we wish to maintain it) is therefore circumstantial and not absolute. It is a given ritual or myth that singles out an opposition by expressing it openly and that thus sets it up as the representative of homologous oppositions.

If we left it at that, the symbolic code would seem like a set of matrices similar to those of the table presented above. But three supplementary properties of symbolic oppositions prevent our being content with such an elementary model. Firstly, a particular element may enter into several oppositions; thus butter on the head is opposed not only to consumed butter, but also to foliage and mosses put on the head during funerary rituals. Secondly, an opposition may have, simultaneously, several values: thus the ritual use of butter is opposed to its use as food not only as is excess to moderation, but also as is cool to hot. Now this second opposition value that plays a fundamental role in Dorze symbolism is realised in a different way – indeed the reverse – in other realms. In the sociological domain, for example, seniors are colder than juniors; in the physiological domain, it is seminal retention which is colder than incontinence, etc. These oppositions inform Dorze symbolic life no less than do those presented in the preceding table. A given opposition therefore figures in several matrices of which it constitutes so to speak the axis of intersection. Thirdly, two homologous oppositions may also be in a relationship of reduction: e.g., take an opposition between two terms A and B. Each of these two terms may itself include two aspects, A1 and A2, and B1 and B2, which are opposed among themselves as A is opposed to B. Thus the alimentary use of butter has two forms, depending on whether it is used in an ordinary meal, where it is used in small quantities, or whether it is used in a ritual feast, in which case it is nearly force-fed. The first form is opposed to the second as the alimentary use of butter generally is opposed to its ritual use, following Figure 1.

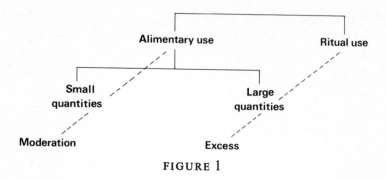

FIGURE 1

On the other hand, the ritual use of butter also has two forms, of which one is relatively moderate – and more common – in which only a piece of butter is placed on the head; the other – much more expensive – and reserved to young married women, in which butter is made into a veritable skullcap. The first form is opposed to the second as the alimentary use of butter is opposed to its ritual use in general, following Figure 2.

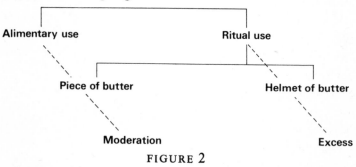

FIGURE 2

This sort of relationship between two oppositions, at once one of homology and of reduction, plays a fundamental role in the analyses of Lévi-Strauss, and further complicates the representation of symbolic systems. We have, thus, the four essential properties of symbolism following the structuralist view: an element does not take on symbolic value except in so far as it is opposed to at least one other element; a symbolic opposition is triply defined: (1) by its domain, (2) by its oppositional values, (3) by its level of reduction. The other properties of symbolism revealed by structural analysis only develop these four fundamental points.

This view, however, poses some serious problems. It must be said – following Lévi-Strauss himself – that the representation of these properties by means of tables, figures, etc., is a convenience of exposition; that the overall structure of the system remains essentially unknown and that we are far from being able to formalise it or explicate it; the model is vague and intuitive; this is a kind of frustration that every anthropologist, for the moment, must share. But above all: what guarantees that the structure outlined accounts for the properties of the object and does not derive simply from the systematising gaze of the analyst? And what *is* this object whose properties will thus be represented?

To the first question, Lévi-Strauss replies by a 'What does it matter?'; '...what does this matter', he says at the beginning of *Mythologiques*, 'for if the final aim of anthropology is to contribute to a better knowledge of objectified thought and its mechanisms, it is in the last resort immaterial whether in this book the thought processes of the South American Indians take shape through the medium of my thought or whether mine take place through the medium of theirs' (Lévi-Strauss 1969: 13). A response which I find enchanting, but not very satisfactory.

I accept that Lévi-Strauss' mind is a proper exemplar of the human mind, and I don't doubt that if, by his work, he revealed its mechanisms, science would have made a considerable leap forward. But just as observing an athlete does not lead to an understanding of muscular physiology, so it is very far from being the case that the exercise of an eminent thought may be its own explanation. A model of the human mind is not confirmed by the fact that it is the product of a human mind for, in that respect, all models – from the most pedestrian to the most fantastical – are equally valid.

Yet I would hold it against myself were I to make Lévi-Strauss sound silly when it is possible to understand him in a completely different way: to consider *Mythologiques* as a deliberate exercise in explicit symbolic thought of which it matters little if it follows the same route as that of the Indians, as long as it reproduces and reveals – even imperfectly – the course of the unconscious. This way, the problem of what this intuitive model might be applicable to is posed in new terms; posed, but not resolved.

The anthropologist must locate the cultural elements that come under symbolic interpretation; so also must the native. He must group and articulate those elements that are to be interpreted together; he must look for and know how to find those elements without which the general articulation is impossible or incomplete; he must determine the abstract schemas by means of which an interpretation becomes possible; so also must the native. In short, the task of the anthropologist in his work, and that of the native in learning his culture, are comparable; with two qualifications. First, the task of the individual in his own culture is achieved in a way that is mostly unconscious; further, we may suppose that the individual does not start from zero, nor advance at random. He has at his disposal in an innate way, certain criteria for selection and data gathering, and certain organising principles for the mechanism which articulates them or, at the least, a learning strategy specifically adapted to the task. The anthropologist, on the contrary, must do it all explicitly and has at his disposal no criterion, no principle, no strategy specific to his objective.

That the anthropologist conceives criteria, principles, a strategy which proves to be efficacious and permits him not only to articulate his materials but also to discover them – is this heuristics and not theory? To the extent that the object of the theory to be made is precisely another heuristic – the unconscious one of the native – the anthropologist is entitled to ask himself if the one is not an imperfect model of the other. The structuralist method falsely presented as a methodology independent of its object is in fact that very heuristic, whose specific efficaciousness suggests the theoretical import.

So far, I have asserted, but certainly not demonstrated, the efficiency of the structuralist method. The table allowed us to show the principles of it, but does not, however, establish its validity. It is clear enough that symbolic phenomena depart from the ordinary, and that they do not depart just in any direction; therefore, there is always a non-symbolic term to which they can be opposed. Scarcely more remarkable is the fact that given an opposition, we find others that correspond to it. Excess and moderation, even if it is not just any excess or moderation, are general enough categories: they may be found to contrast in many domains without this being a great discovery. The same is true for most abstract symbolic oppositions found in the literature: up–down, cold–hot, feminine–masculine, right–left, nature–culture, etc. As in the case of Freudian symbolism, we are still at the level of a trivial party game. However, many societies do play this game, dividing things without laterality into left and right (see Needham 1973), and things without verticality into up and down. Thus the Dorze divide the whole universe into cool and hot and into senior and junior (see Sperber 1974), following principles I must have internalised intuitively since – I repeatedly tested this – I apply them as they do, without being able yet to make them explicit.

The reduction of symbolic oppositions is already a bit less expected. For example, that there are two modes of ritual use of butter, so be it. But that they are opposed as are excess and moderation – that is to say as are ritual use and alimentary use – is more interesting. But only a bit more, for though we could cite many analogous examples, we could foresee clearly neither the existence, nor the specific form, of a reduced opposition.

But accepting the model entails other, more remarkable consequences. In the examples of symbolic oppositions given so far, one of the terms was marked with relation to the other. When a Dorze eats a normally buttered dish, no symbolism need be postulated. But if there is a large quantity of butter, this marked use points up the opposition between an ordinary meal and a feast. If butter is put on the head in a normal quantity, the opposition to culinary use is implicit; in turn, it takes the buttery skullcap of the young married woman to evoke the opposition between the two ritual uses whose second term only is marked. In other words, an element takes on its symbolic value to the extent that it departs from a norm, a norm which may, itself, be symbolic. If this departure is constitutive of symbolism, and not accessory or fortuitous, two consequences are foreseeable. Firstly, the direction of the departure should be relevant for, after all, there are at least fifty ways of not consuming butter normally. The existence of a series of departures operating in the same direction, and thus homologous among themselves, realises – but too vaguely – this first consequence.

Secondly, if the marked term of a symbolic opposition is located in a relevant direction, then in principle the reverse direction should also be relevant. It should determine a symbolic element opposed to the first, no longer this time, as a marked term to a non-marked term, but following a symmetrical inversion between the two terms located on both sides of a third, non-marked, term.

Take, again, the example of butter on the head. It is defined as a non-consumption of the food *par excellence*. Therefore it gives us occasion to look for the reverse – a case of consumption of the non-food *par excellence*, for example, coprophagy. But it would not suffice on the one hand to find a non-consumption of butter, and on the other, coprophagy, to be assured that contrasting them is not the ethnographer's own doing, but rather proceeds from Dorze symbolism itself. As butter on the head marks a social status, we would need to find that coprophagy, for example, marked a contrasting status.

We have seen that buttered dignitaries contrast with big sacrificers. Both are guarantors of fertility, do not cut their hair, cannot leave the country, etc. But while the position of dignitary is transitory, that of sacrificer is permanent. The one obliges its holder to make multiple gifts, while the other makes its holder receive them. The one is linked with public places, roads, forums and markets, the other with groves, forests, fields. The one makes a show, the other keeps himself apart from all agitation. The dignitary has a right to the most dramatic funerary rites in a public field; the sacrificer, alone among all the Dorze, has no other funerary rites than those at his home. Accession to the title of sacrificer does not include transition rituals, a tour of the market place or butter on the head. Yet – the sacrificer must swallow a part of the contents of the intestine of a slaughtered animal, that is to say, its wrapped-up liquid excrement, as opposed to the solid butter that the dignitary wears, open to the air, on his head. The sacrificer shows thereby – and this time the commentary is Dorze – what he is ready to swallow for the sake of his people. Inversely, the dignitary shows the point to which he is willing to renounce food.

Another thing. I knew that several Dorze rituals included a ceremonial tour (of the market place or of a public field), always oriented from right to left; therefore, I looked for one instance at least of a tour in the other direction, which would have clarified, contrastively, the status of the one who made the tour. For a long time, I was unsuccessful.

Furthermore, one of the last days of the big annual ritual at *Mask'al* ends with a very special sacrifice: the highest-ranking dignitary slits the throat of a bull at the market place; all the spectators keep their distance. Scarcely does the animal begin to bleed, when the dignitary hurries away and all the spectators throw a hail of stones sometimes lasting for an hour, until an audacious person, braving the projectiles, goes up to the beast, which thereupon belongs to him. This inaccessible food suggested I should look, inversely, for a form of unusually easy access to food.

I was thus searching for two apparently unrelated symbolic elements. Aided by structuralist faith, here is what I found. Three years before my arrival in the field, the incumbent of a singular office – that of official beggar at the market – died, without an heir. This beggar (who, incidentally, was not particularly poor) could, the whole year round, demand foodstuffs of all the merchants without risking a refusal which would have brought them misfortune. The morning of the sacrifice outlined above, he too sacrificed a bull in the same place and, as soon as the animal was slaughtered, he rushed off, making a tour of the market place *from left to right*, under a volley of cow dung. Thus we have an opposition between the classical ceremonial tour, done from right to left and causing the merchants to flee the area, and a tour done in the other direction while fleeing the spectators. One between excessively easy access to all the commodities in the market, for a single individual, and excessively difficult access for all to a single slaughtered animal. One between a hail of hard projectiles deterring approach and a hail of soft projectiles forcing movement. A contrast between the dignitary, honoured provider of the community, and the official beggar, amply provided for but made ridiculous. Finally, there is a contrast between the ordinary role of each of these characters and their extraordinary role on this day: the one provided for becoming the provider, and the animal sacrificed by the provider being denied to the community.

These two cases suggest a turn about and confirm the

connection between butter and excrement, at the same time showing that it should be made not under the sign of identity, but under that of symbolic inversion – the consumption of excrement opposed to the non-consumption of butter, and ritual anticlockwise tour of the market place with butter on one's head, opposed to a tour in the opposite direction with excrement on the body. Also possible is a return to the problem of exegesis: here is a set of facts that the natives abstain almost totally from commenting upon without thereby making it impossible to interpret. The third type of meaning envisaged by Turner, 'positional meaning' which derives from the relation of symbolic phenomena among themselves in a symbolic system, constitutes a primal principle of interpretation whereas the other two types of meaning – exegetical and operational – merely extend the object to be interpreted (cf. Turner 1967: 50–1).

Larger systems with fuller examples are to be found in *Mythologiques* and in other works, such as that which Marcel Detienne has devoted to the mythology of aromatics in Greece, *Les jardins d'Adonis* (1972). These works show not only the existence of systematic symbolic inversions, but also their relevance. They do not derive merely from an *a posteriori* organisation of already-assembled materials but, on the contrary, permit the *a priori* formulation of certain hypotheses and the discovery – in the field or in texts – of materials predicted by the analysis. From the point of view of the scholar who adopts such a method, this sort of inversion is too beautiful to be fortuitous, this sort of success too satisfying for him not carefully to concern himself with the systematic underlying properties that make it possible.

A personal conviction does not equal an argument, and we must consider the sceptic's reservations: 'Given the way you formulate your hypotheses, how can they be falsified?

You only take account of your successes, not of your failures. When you fail, you don't question your general hypotheses, you only question their immediate application and you go off in another direction, guided as much or more by your flair as by your pseudo-theory. Other scholars before you have known how to winkle out and relate symbolic facts without mistaking their methods for that of the human mind itself. Conversely, several unimaginative structuralists have applied the principles you invoke to the letter, and have only come up with a string of sententious platitudes. If one were to give a structuralist a list of fifty words taken at random, he would be quick to see in them a pretty set of oppositions and structural inversions, and would set them out in elegant matrices, while another in his own way would arrive at an equally harmonious result which would be completely different. In sum, you have merely invented a party game which is a little more subtle than that of the cryptologists or the Freudians (and yet the latter have developed theirs since the texts you cite were published). But a theory? Even the outline of an hypothesis? Nonsense!'

These are not bad arguments. In any case, no worse than those commonly given in favour of the structuralist method. Thus it may be useful to answer them carefully.

First, we must distinguish two levels. On the one hand, the general principles that underlie the structuralist method, and on the other, the particular analyses which derive from it. These general principles – the sceptic is right – are not falsifiable, and therefore do not constitute a theory. Rather, it is a question, as I have already said, of a vague heuristic, or, of a reasoned flair, which amounts to the same thing. This heuristic works well. But since we do not know what symbolism would have to be like for it not to work, it does not tell us anything about what symbolism is not, nor consequently, about what it is.

If it is hard to conceive of a form of symbolism which

would lie outside the scope of this heuristic, it is easy to think of other heuristics which cannot account for symbolism at all. We have seen several such examples in the preceding chapters. The structuralist method has at least the merit of giving every least element its place and thus of considerably enlarging the stock of relevant data. Suppose, for example, that we were content to explain butter on the head by saying that it visibly separates the participants in rituals of transition from the rest of the Dorze. In this way, one might account for the presence of a marker, but the fact that it is butter, that it is worn on the head, etc., remains completely arbitrary; a special hat, or a bit of red paint on the nose could serve as well. If we explain it as a symbolic equivalent of semen (in so far as this is an explanation), the presence of a whitish substance ceases to be arbitrary, but ten other substances could have done as well and – a consideration which is not a matter of indifference to the Dorze – most of them would be much less expensive. On the other hand, in the fragments of structuralist description I have offered, everything is based on the fact that it is butter which is at issue. Replace it with a hat or with wheat pap, and the analysis collapses.

If the stock of the relevant data is thus considerably enlarged, the price we pay for this enlarging is equally great. All previous analyses of symbolism articulate their data following the positive criteria of resemblance and contiguity (cf. Smith and Sperber 1971). In adding the negative criteria of opposition and inversion the structuralist gives himself the means of establishing many new relevant relationships and of including in his schemas – under one heading or another – any element at all. Moreover, as the criteria are applied in an intuitive and uncertain manner, the new instrument is much too powerful. The price of this success seems to be that the structuralist, from then on, cannot fail.

Thus it is, at least, on the level of general principles. This is what the sceptic is asserting when he says that from an arbitrary list of fifty words we can make one, or even several, structural descriptions. This is quite true, with one qualification: either the analyst will consider these fifty terms as the complete universe of his description, and not all the terms will be relevant, some only finding a place as redundant equivalents of others, or else he will consider them as a sample of a larger set and will manage to give relevance to each given element by bringing to bear hypothetical ones.

Imagine, then, two structural descriptions of such a list which would be different but equally good, in the sense that they both give relevance to each element. Now add a fifty-first element. For a given structural description, either this additional element will have a ready-made place, or else the new set must be the object of a new description. If the first fifty elements constitute a sample of a larger set which both descriptions must account for, and if one and not the other of these descriptions allows the accommodation of the new element, then this additional datum corroborates one description and falsifies the other.

In practice, structuralist descriptions of symbolism are never done on closed sets: either because the data are fragmentary (and when are they not?), or because the analyst is not initially working on the whole of his data but only on a fraction of it, checking or modifying his description as he goes along. Note that the position of the native *vis-à-vis* his own culture is identical: he is not confronted all at once by the whole set of myths, rites, etc., nor required to make an immutable representation of it. Thus, the analogy to a puzzle which is often made is misleading: in a well-made puzzle, all the pieces remain the same forever, and for each, there is only one 'solution'. Structural analysis allows several solutions but eliminates some as it goes along. There are good reasons for thinking that the native here again proceeds in the same way.

66

The example of an arbitrary list of fifty words invoked by the sceptic to make fun of the structuralist method turns back on him, for a first time. If it is true that several structural descriptions are possible, there are, in principle, good empirical arguments for preferring one description and throwing out another. Once a heuristic not only enlarges the stock of relevant data but also contains a criterion for evaluating the empirical import of differing descriptions, this heuristic incorporates not only know-how, but also actual knowledge which should then be explicated.

The example of the arbitrary list served, in the sceptic's mind, a further purpose to show that the method is applicable not only to symbolism but to anything at all, to the cultural as well as the accidental, to information as well as noise, in short, that it enlarges the stock of relevant data much too far. But here the sceptic has not reflected enough on the properties of symbolism and of any theory which could account for it. Or is he, too, a victim of the semiological illusion? Presented to the faithful as the ultimate message of their prophet, this arbitrary list would at once take on a symbolic value that would by extension apply to each of its elements. In fact, arbitrariness is one of the means of symbolic production: e.g., a collection of ordinary objects transformed into relics, pebbles tossed at random and interpreted by divination, surrealist experiments in automatic writing, etc. Symbolic thought is capable, precisely, of transforming noise into information; no code, by definition, would be able to do this. Any model of symbolism is inadequate if it is not capable of the same feat, and the sceptic's example once again is turned against him.

In short, the structuralist works following intuitions which are partly explicit. The predictive value of his approach assures him that the structures he outlines do not derive solely from his systematising perception, but that they account – at least a little – for the properties of the object under scrutiny. Or, which amounts to the same thing, that his partially explicated intuitions more or less match the unconscious intuitions that are the basis of symbolism itself. Yet, if the anthropologist is reassured as to the value of his particular analyses, and ready, in principle, to put forward, on the basis of the success of his approach, some more general hypotheses, one would still like to know what object these hypotheses might be about.

Indeed, a system of homologies, oppositions and inversions is, in itself, mysterious enough. It is hard to see in what sense it explains or interprets symbolic phenomena. It organises them. But what is the role, what is the nature of this organisation? Failing to answer this question, one leaves oneself open to the reproach of having constructed a model without an object. The reply that Lévi-Strauss makes – i.e., that this object is a semiological system, a structure that articulates signs – does not satisfy me.

If we accept – for purposes of testing it – the hypothesis which states that the device underlying both the ethnographer's approach and symbolic thought generally is a code, the first question to be answered is, where are the pairs (message, interpretation) or (signifier, signified)?

The matrices we have outlined offer for each symbolic opposition, a surplus of possible interpretations. For the following equation:

$$\text{alimentary use of butter : ritual butter :: } x : y$$

the opposition $(x:y)$ may be replaced by all the values of the opposition of the two uses of butter: (moderation : excess), (hot : cold); and there are others. We might therefore consider the interpretation of one opposition as the set (or a subset, or one) of its values; the interpretation would be an abstract form of the opposition. When Lévi-Strauss suggests for the opposition (raw : cooked) and (nakedness : attire), the interpretation (nature : culture), it is definitely a case of an abstraction of this sort.

The opposition $(x : y)$ may also be replaced by the set (or the subset or one) of the oppositions that have the same value as (alimentary butter : ritual butter), for example, (commercial activity in the market : ceremonial tour), (constipation : purge). In this case, the interpretation would be of the same level of abstraction as the message, and the role of the shared abstract value would be to associate them. Thus, when Lévi-Strauss (1962) analyses so-called totemism by showing that the opposition between two animal totems refers back to the opposition between two human clans, the interpretation of an opposition in the zoological domain is an homologous opposition in the sociological domain. In this particular example, the value of the opposition may be nothing more than the distinctiveness between groups: a natural one between animal species, a cultural one between human clans. Or else more specific oppositional values may be used: aquatic animals opposed to terrestrial animals as a clan of fishers to a clan of hunters, for instance.

We may thus view symbolic matrices as sets of possible interpretations for each of the oppositions that figure in them; the choice of interpretation of a particular occurrence of a symbolic element would depend on contextual data. This model is analogous to that of a multi-lingual dictionary: we may consult it to find the meaning of a particular word (cf. the abstract value of a particular opposition), or to find a word having the same meaning in another language (cf. an opposition having the same value in another domain).

But Lévi-Strauss rightfully refuses to use these matrices as a set of terms among which to choose. For if at a given moment in the analysis an underlying opposition (abstract or not), homologous to a manifest opposition, takes on a particular importance, it neither exhausts nor even constitutes its interpretation. Firstly, the other homologies are kept in reserve and not abandoned, contrary to what happens in language when a choice is made between the meanings of an ambiguous word. Secondly, the underlying opposition which is focussed upon does not substitute for the manifest opposition to which it is homologous, but rather is articulated to it, unlike what happens when an interpretation is substituted for a message.

Despite some statements to the contrary, symbolism conceived in this way is not a means of encoding information, but a means of organising it. A symbolic opposition must not be replaced by an interpretation, but placed in an organisation of which it constitutes a crucial element.

Thus, the problem for a Dorze is not to choose an interpretation for butter on the head according to the ritual context, but to organise his mental image of ritual and of social life in general in such a way that butter will find its place within it. The opposition of ritual use of butter to its alimentary use, the existence of homologous oppositions brought together by diverse rituals and texts, contributes to the formation of a coherent schema of Dorze ritual and social life. Butter will have served as an index for selecting some hypotheses which other indices corroborate. In other words, in contrast to what happens in a semiological decoding, it is not a question of interpreting symbolic phenomena by means of a context, but – quite the contrary – of interpreting the context by means of symbolic phenomena. Those who try to interpret symbols in and of themselves look at the light source and say, 'I don't see anything.' But the light source is there, not to be looked at, but so that one may look at what it illuminates. The same goes for symbolism.

The idea that symbolic elements organise the mental representation of systems of which they are parts is clearly suggested when, in the first chapter of *The Savage Mind*, Lévi-Strauss compares mythical thought to *bricolage*. The *bricoleur* gathers objects, various odds and ends of which he may always make something but never just anything; for each element, once one wishes to utilise it, suggests some plans and rejects others, just as each symbolic element suggests some interpretations not of itself, but of the set in which it finds its place. Of this symbolic '*bricolage*', the very text of Lévi-Strauss gives an involuntary example for the author insists on using in it the notion of *signification* (translated in English in Lévi-Strauss 1966 as 'signification' but meaning nothing else than 'meaning') and can only do so by changing it: '[The *bricoleur*] interrogates all the heterogeneous objects of which his treasury is composed to discover what each of them could "signify" and so contribute to the definition of a set which has yet to materialise' (Lévi-Strauss 1966: 18 [the quotation marks around 'signify' are Lévi-Strauss' own]). And, contrasting 'concept' with 'signification' he says, 'Concepts thus appear like operators *opening up* the set being worked with and signification like the operator of its *reorganization*' (Lévi-Strauss 1966: 20). A definition which may work for symbolism, but surely not for *signification*.

And in *The Raw and the Cooked*: 'The layered structure of myth to which I draw attention... allows us to look upon myth as a matrix of meanings which are arranged in lines or columns, but in which each level always refers to some other level, whichever way the myth is read. Similarly, each matrix of meanings refers to another matrix, each myth to other myths. And if it is now asked to what final meaning these mutually significative meanings are referring – since in the last resort and in their totality they must refer to something – the only reply to emerge from this study is that myths signify the mind that evolves by making use of the world of which it is itself a part. Thus there is simultaneous production of myths themselves, by the mind that generates them and, by myths, of an image of the world which is already inherent in the structure of the mind' (Lévi-Strauss 1969: 341).

As these quotations show, for Lévi-Strauss meaning is not a concept, but a symbol, and he never uses it without 'bricolating' it a bit, without giving it a mytho-poetic quality it only acquires precisely in losing all precise meaning.

The same applies for the notion of language. In the four volumes of *Mythologiques*, Lévi-Strauss analyses a set of myths of the Indians of both Americas and shows that these myths are related to each other. Not only does the same thematic underlie them, not only are they developed on similar frames, but moreover, they maintain relations of structural proximity which only in part reflect either geographical or historical proximity. We might be tempted to see in these *Mythologiques* the description of a language of which each Indian society knows only bits which have finally been reassembled by Lévi-Strauss. A splendid metaphor which some accept to the letter: since myths arise from the human mind and form this language that no one speaks, then this human mind is the mind of no one, a metaphysical entity, similar to the Hegelian universal Mind whose inventor would be himself the incarnation of it – Hegel and Napoleon at one and the same time. I do not know how this interpretation, could have been arrived at. In my view, Lévi-Strauss' purpose has less grandeur but more import.

Of his own culture and of neighbouring ones, the native generally knows more myths than does the anthropologist, and knows them better. The references are clear to him and few allusions escape him. To understand them, he has available a multitude of indices, for symbolism is an everyday affair. The anthropologist, on the contrary, must write everything down painfully, translate it all, verify it all. In the final analysis, he has only scraps at his disposal. Often he works on a colleague's cold materials, which speak little and don't answer at all. In these conditions, and because he doesn't see much, the anthropologist is entitled to look further afield.

He is entitled firstly, because he might suppose that the symbolisms of different peoples differ more in their representation than in their rules. When, for example, a myth includes an episode whose role is obscure, and the myth of another people, analogous to it in structure, develops more clearly a similar or inverse episode and clarifies its function, therein lies the basis of an hypothesis.

An example. I collected, in Dorze, a myth which may be summarised as follows: A man whose step-mother has emasculated him saves the daughter of a king by killing by fire the monstrous serpent to whom she has been given up. The king rewards him by giving him his daughter in marriage, but, having heard rumour about the misfortune of his son-in-law, he organises a public bathing party to reassure himself. Just as he joins the bathers, the hero sees a gazelle, and escapes by pretending to pursue it. When he is just at the point of killing it, Mariam, 'The Lady', appears before him, begs him to spare the animal, and in exchange, gives him new virility.

In this highly structured story, a detail nevertheless left me perplexed: why do all the narrators insist that the hero was emasculated by a step-mother who is never mentioned again? A dual hypothesis was suggested to me by a variant collected by Moreno among the Galla of Ethiopia. A young girl is disguised as a man and sent to war by her father, who is excessively proud of her. She attracts notice in combat and the king gives her his own daughter in marriage. But having been warned of the sex of his 'son-in-law' he organises a public bathing party to reassure himself. The heroine is saved *in extremis* by Mariam who lends her virility (Moreno 1935: 48–54).

A quick glance at these two texts reveals a dual inversion: on the one hand a father who elevates his daughter to manhood, and a step-mother who deprives her step-son of his, both departing from the norm according to which a girl, no matter how well loved, cannot succeed her father, while a step-son, no matter how hated, is nevertheless his father's heir and takes precedence over the children of a second wife. An inversion, on the other hand, between a victorious woman warrior, that is to say (in this cultural context), a woman who emasculates men, and a man emasculated far from the battlefield by a woman: two terms situated on either side of the norm that states that only men emasculate and are emasculated and uniquely in the context of battle.

Establishing this dual inversion is enough to reveal certain themes that are shared by Dorze and Galla symbolic systems. But, as far as I know, the Dorze do not know the Galla version and the hypothesis suggested by the comparison must be verified through examination of Dorze data alone. Among the Dorze, there is a status of killer which may be acquired either by killing a wild animal (a lion, leopard or rhinoceros, for example) and by cutting off its tail, or by killing a man in warfare and cutting off his penis. This status is the only one that is open to any man regardless of birth, and which is neither directly nor indirectly inherited. It is marked by the customary tour of the market place with butter on the head, and by spectacular funerary rites.

If we now return to the Dorze myth, we see that it is not concerned with warfare except by an underlying opposition between the domestic context of the castration of the hero and the military context which alone would be sanctioned by the norm. Neither does it concern real hunting, except that by killing a serpent by fire, which is a dual transgression of taboo, the hero places himself above it, and in attacking a gazelle, the hero places himself below it, taking each time for his target animals whose death does not give their killer the status of 'killer'. But as these oppositions suggest, it is not by chance that all these elements of the myth are placed in opposition to this central absent term formed by the status of killer and the warfare and hunting which are necessary to it. This absent term is in a way the very theme of the myth. The apparently gratuitous detail of the castrating step-mother evokes and doubly clarifies the status of killer – on the one hand by inversion, on the other directly, by showing that the killer *par excellence* is a non-heir who is in search of a penis: the principle of descent outside of descent. Many other endogenous data suggest this interpretation to the Dorze auditor, but the ethnographer only finds them because an exogenous datum – the Galla version, which is unknown to the Dorze – shows him the way.

It is never necessary, and it is even sometimes impossible, to formulate an hypothesis by means of only those data which would allow its validation. This distinction between two uses of materials is not limited to the study of symbolism. Here is a linguistic example of it. In the Marseillais dialect of French, the feminine form of the adjective is clearly marked by a suffix /ə/, as in 'petite maison', where one hears the final 'e' of the adjective. The presence of this vocalic suffix allows a simple description of the phenomena of elision and liaison. In Parisian pronunciation, no vocalic suffix phonetically marks the feminine form, and the rules of elision and of liaison therefore seem more complex. But the example from Marseillais suggests to the linguist that he should hypothesise the existence in Parisian of an unpronounced vocalic suffix, corresponding to the famous 'silent e', which would greatly simplify his description. Other characteristics of Parisian will validate such an hypothesis (cf. Dell 1973, part 2) which is more obvious in Marseillais where it is based on immediately perceptible evidence and not on a phenomenon whose reality remains underlying – phonological, but not phonetic.

In any case, and even if the hypothesis is discovered by means of the data of Marseillais, it is only the data of Parisian which allow one to validate it. The reason is that even a Parisian who has never heard Marseillais may and must construct in his internalised grammar the simple rules of elision and of liaison, and he can only do this by means of Parisian. Linguistics can only validate its hypotheses in terms of the data actually used by the native speaker, precisely because there are hypotheses about the mental mechanism of that speaker. Similarly, because the symbolic mechanism the Dorze use to interpret myth is a mental one, we cannot validate the model of it except by means of data that are available to them, even if other data have suggested the model in the first place.

However, the comparison of myths of different peoples has other justifications than its suggestive power. Indeed, when the anthropologist proceeds in this way, he is really only following the example of the natives themselves. The ethnographic literature shows that the men of one society often listen to the myths of their neighbours, and that they compare them to their own in order to create new ones.

Thus, the Dorze and the Galla belong to two language groups which are only distantly related. We can probably exclude the supposition that the myth in question derives from a hypothetical era when they had a common language, and that the two versions diverged at the same time as the languages did, if only because the episode with Mariam witnesses a much more recent borrowing from Ethiopian Orthodox Christianity. Two other hypotheses seem more realistic: either that the one group was inspired by the other at a time when they were more closely in contact, or that both were inspired, directly or indirectly, by the same third source. Now, what is striking, anyhow, is that the differences between the two versions are no less systematic than are the similarities. In other words, that the borrowing of a myth is not simply a departure which, with time, arbitrarily becomes more distant from its model, but rather it is a set of rule-governed transformations: there is identity in the case of the three episodes of marriage with the king's daughter, the public bathing party, and the intervention of Mariam. There is paired suppression, in the Galla version, of the two episodes with the serpent and the gazelle – that is to say, of these two anti-hunts – which are replaced by exploits of warfare accomplished by an anti-warrior. There is transformation by inversion in the initial episode: young woman raised by a man and elevated to manhood status, as against young man deprived by a woman of his virility. In the one case, a positive abuse of a relation of descent; in the other case, a negative abuse of a relation of affinity, to the detriment of descent.

The fact of borrowing, in matters of symbolism, therefore has more than merely a comparative or historical interest. The systematic transformations which accompany these borrowings suggest hypotheses concerning the nature of symbolism itself, if only because they are related to inversions characteristic of a symbolic system viewed from the inside. Thus, the Dorze myth is in certain respects a transformation of the Galla one, and in other respects it is a transformation of the set of practices and rules that define the status of killer; and it is the first sort of transformation that allows the discovery of the second.

An hypothesis then comes to mind: the symbolic interpretation of myth and ritual which an individual may come to know in his own culture would consist in abstracting from them a more general structure that other myths and other rituals, opposed to them, would realise as well, were it not that a second level of interpretation – this time ideological – dictates our adherence to the ones and our neglect or refusal of the others. Belief in myth and ritual would constitute not the first principle, but a second development of their symbolic value. If such an hypothesis were taken up, we could conceive that in moving from one culture to another, ideology would change radically, but symbolism only superficially; we could conceive that the individual object of symbolic interpretation is for a large part transculturally defined; that each culture gives it only a particular realisation, sufficient for the individual unconsciously to reconstruct the principle behind it, while the anthropologist, having available to him bits only, must assemble them on a broader scale in order to arrive at the same result.

The symbolisms of two related societies are certainly not identical, but it is possible that they overlap and that they differ more in their manifest forms than in the principles that underlie them. To the extent that these principles constitute the object of learning for the individual, as well as the object of study for the anthropologist, it matters little that they succeed by means of the same evidence.

This hypothesis is attractive. It is not very clear and lacks confirmation. One would have to establish, on the one hand, that these transcultural principles exist, and on the other, that it is really they that individuals internalise. Lévi-Strauss' work in *Mythologiques* bears only on the first point. He shows clearly, albeit in an intuitive fashion, that there are systematic relationships of transformation between myths separated in space and also differing in form. But these transformations are revealed in a *Gedankenexperiment*, and generally do not correspond to the actual transformations that would have accompanied direct borrowing. It is not even certain, nor asserted moreover, that they necessarily result from a series of borrowings for as is shown by some comparisons between Greek and Amerindian myths, for example, the same structure may appear in two parts of the world without our having to assume that they are related.

Although it is a mental experiment which by itself merely demonstrates its own possibility, *Mythologiques* suggests, nevertheless, a treasure trove of ethnographic hypotheses which concern Americanists and, also, two general theoretical hypotheses: firstly, that the logic of actual borrowing is the same as that of mental transformations; secondly, that the logic behind the formation of myths and the logic behind their transformations are the same.

A society's myths have two origins – one, the transformation of other myths, endogenous or exogenous, the other, the transformation into myth of data of another kind. Both are well attested, for example, in the Indo-European studies that Georges Dumézil has carried out. Imagine, for example, an historical narrative transmitted orally in a non-literate society. Unless a concerted effort were made to preserve it in its initial form, certain episodes would soon be forgotten, while others would be magnified; the whole – here impoverished, there enriched – would acquire a more regular structure, a greater symbolic import, a memorableness that the original did not have; in short, it is transformed into a culturally exemplary, psychologically salient object which, once adopted by a society, becomes – precisely – a myth (cf. Sperber 1973). This process of mnemonic and symbolic selection together is observable in a more condensed form in the transmission of rumours as well as in the remembering of personal experience (cf. Pierre Smith 1973). History itself – not that studied by professionals, but that retained by each of us – does not find itself any the less affected. Here is an example of it taken from Edmund Leach (Leach 1966a: 100):

'For a contemporary English schoolboy, the really memorable facts about English sixteenth-century history are details such as the following:

(a) Henry VIII was a very successful masculine King who married many wives and murdered several of them;

(b) Edward VI was a very feeble masculine King who remained a virgin until his death;

(c) Mary Queen of Scots was a very unsuccessful female King who married many husbands and murdered several of them;

(d) Queen Elizabeth was a very successful female King who remained a virgin until her death...'

Thus, the memorableness of a text seems to depend on a structure made up of homologies and inversions that the wear and tear of memory, and better still, oral transmission, confers upon it if it does not possess it to begin with. And we might, with Lévi-Strauss, admit 'that all literary, oral, or written creation can, at the beginning, only be individual. But once it is given over to oral tradition as the latter is produced among non-literate peoples, only structured levels that are based on shared foundations remain stable, while probabilistic levels will manifest an extreme variability, itself a function of the personalities of successive narrators. However, in the course of the process of oral transmission, these probabilistic levels run into each other. They thus wear each other down, progressively laying bare what one might call the crystalline core of the body of speech. Individual works are all potential myths, but it is their collective adoption that actualises – if such should be the case – their "mythicism" ' (Lévi-Strauss 1971: 560).

If the formation of myths consists precisely in giving them such a regular structure, once they have it, why transform them? Why not adopt, without changing a line, the neighbours' myths which – if they were good enough for them in this regard, should be good enough for others? Because this structure exists not only at the level of the isolated myth, but also – or especially – at that of the corpus of myths that are transmitted in a society, at the very level of the symbolism as a whole whose myths – properly so-called – are only one of its manifestations. The transformations have the effect precisely of integrating an exogenous myth into this ensemble; but this integration is never so perfect that it is not still necessary the better to unite them, to transform the endogenous myths as well. With the result that the search for an unattainable equilibrium is translated into constant change.

According to such a view, it is the same properties that make myths both memorable and transformable. The study of their transformations is not distinct from that of their own structure; they both uncover systematic relations of homology and inversion both within and between myths, both within a corpus and between one corpus and another.

But if the anthropologist can view as similar these relations of internal or external transformations, they present themselves to the native under two vastly different lights. On the one hand, there are potential transformations between synchronically given elements of a corpus which the native may reconstruct mentally in an unconscious manner; on the other, there are actual transformations, diachronically arranged, and which, precisely because they really took place, are missing one of the terms so that they cannot be reconstructed in the mind.

It is in this sense that Lévi-Strauss, in *Mythologiques*, performs an artificial mental experiment: he treats as a synchronically given set myths which no one before him had ever envisaged *en bloc*, myths not found side by side in any culture, but only in Americanist libraries. Some critics argue from the artificiality of the object treated to the vacuousness of hypotheses about it. Others, on the contrary, argue from the strength of these hypotheses to the reality of the object, the existence of this famous language which would be constituted by myths across cultures. These attitudes both seem equally poorly founded to me.

Once again, it is not at all necessary that the materials that have led to the development of an hypothesis suffice to validate it, and so the object of *Mythologiques* may be artificial without its hypotheses therefore being empty. To corroborate them, it would be necessary to study mythology and symbolism within a society and not to look beyond except to the extent that its own members do. This is the direction of research that most of Lévi-Strauss' students are following today. We may ask ourselves then if it would not have been possible to begin there, to obviate an apparent detour. We may imagine a Lévi-Strauss who would have stayed for several years in one society and would have studied its myths from within to arrive at a similar view. It matters little. The study of myths has passed through the mental experiment of *Mythologiques* to its greatest benefit. It does not displease me that a rigourless discipline like ours can, as though in compensation, submit thus to the mark of individual genius.

The validity of a set of hypotheses is independent of the data that permitted its formulation; conversely, this validity does not guarantee that the set of these data constitutes an autonomous entity. We may accept the view of myths proposed by Lévi-Strauss without being bound to accept that the set of Amerindian myths is part of the selfsame language. Actually, if this were not the case, one would encounter an irresolvable paradox.

A grammar is a device that generates the sentences of the language it describes by means of given axioms and by the operation of rules, independently of all external input. All sentences, the whole language, are contained in its grammar. Conversely, according to Lévi-Strauss, myths are generated by the transformation of other myths or of texts which carry a certain mythicism; in other words, by a device that allows an infinite and non-enumerable set of possible inputs. No grammar therefore generates by itself the set of myths, any more than the mechanism of visual perception generates by itself the set of possible perceptions. The device that would generate myths depends on an external stimulus; it is thus similar to cognitive devices and opposed to semiological devices: it is an interpretative, and not a generative, system.

Lévi-Strauss has demonstrated the opposite of what he asserts, and myths do not constitute a language. He proposed the first elaborated alternative to semiological views of myth – and, beyond that of symbolism – all the while stating that he was, above all else, a semiologist.

Lévi-Strauss says that 'the universe of primitives (or those claimed to be such) consists principally of messages' (Lévi-Strauss 1964: 353–4). In fact, it is the universe of the French, and more generally, of Westerners, that consists of messages. In current usage, any object of knowledge has, perforce, a sense, a meaning – from the meaning of life to the meaning of the colour of leaves in the autumn. To say that a phenomenon has no meaning is to avow that nothing at all can be said of it. The Frenchman lives in a universe where everything means something, where every correlation is a relation of meaning, where the cause is the sign of its effect and the effect, a sign of its cause. By a singular inversion, only real signs – words, texts – are said, sometimes, to mean nothing at all.

But this semiologism, though it is found in other cultures as well, is in no way universal. For the Dorze, for example, the question 'What does that mean?' (*awa yusi?*) can only be asked about a word, a sentence, a text or a directly paraphrasable behaviour, such as a nod. Even when a natural phenomenon is considered as the effect of a supernatural will, it is not counted as meaning it. In short, if the Dorze universe 'consists principally of messages' they know nothing of it, nor do I.

The attribution of sense is an essential aspect of symbolic development in *our* culture. Semiologism is one of the

83

bases of *our* ideology. For centuries, this semiologism has, tacitly and undividedly, dominated symbolic production. It is less surprising therefore that those whose work for the first time questions this domination expressly render it a first and last homage. If they feel a need to call themselves semiologists, it is to hide – from themselves as well as others – the fact that they have ceased to be such, that they don't know which sign to avow.

Soon it will be for semiology as it was for evolutionism. Once we saw that it was no longer necessary to take as gospel the declarations of the founders of contemporary anthropology or to see in the social forms they described the stages of a unilinear evolution, we realised at once that they had forged the conceptual tools for synchronic description of society and of culture. Similarly, when we strip the work of Lévi-Strauss of the semiological burden with which he has chosen to encumber it, we will then realise that he was the first to propose the fundamentals of an analysis of symbolism which was finally freed from the absurd idea that symbols mean. The argument may be summarised in this way: if symbols had a meaning, it would be obvious enough. All these learned terms – signifier and signified, paradigm and syntagm, code, mytheme will not for long hide the following paradox: that if Lévi-Strauss thought of myths as a semiological system, the myths thought themselves in him, and without his knowledge, as a cognitive system.

4

Symbolism and Knowledge

Symbols are not signs. They are not paired with their interpretations in a code structure. Their interpretations are not meanings.

What little relevance there is in the resemblances between symbolism and language has been exhausted. We must now concentrate on the differences between them, those properties of symbolism that were hidden by the semiological view. These are many and important. Here, I shall only investigate the most general of them. They will suffice to limit considerably the range of possible theories of symbolism.

The individual, in constructing his grammar or his symbolic mechanism, selects among empirical data those that are relevant to his purpose, that is to say, he takes sounds that he does not yet understand to be speech, and phenomena he is not yet able to interpret to be symbolic. In the case of language, the relevant data have a certain homogeneity which is lacking in the case of symbolism; it is easy enough to give an approximate definition of what is speech and what is not and linguistics generally takes this definition as given. Similarly, no child with the gift of hearing makes the mistake of trying to construct his grammar out of visual or kinesthetic data. By contrast, the first problem for a theory of symbolism is to delimit the data relevant to it, and the first problem for the child is to delimit what will be processed symbolically.

Speech is information that is not, in reality, confused with

85

any other sort. It uses the auditory canal and has a specific organisation. For symbolism things are different. Information may come through any or all of the senses. Symbolic information has no identifiable systematic properties.

In some cultures, a part of the symbolic material is clearly isolated, e.g., initiation rites, or rituals performed and myths told in a way that clearly contrasts with daily life. But such special treatment is not universal; in some societies myths are told with no more care than village gossip, and rites performed with scarcely any more care or fervour than are practical activities. But whether or not the indices that mark as symbolic certain practices and texts are striking or discreet, they only have value for those who can recognise them. Yet these indices are in no way explicit; they do not expressly mean 'interpret what follows symbolically', but, rather, must themselves be symbolically interpreted. If we add to this that these indices mark off only a part of the symbolic material, we see that the problem of data selection in terms of which learning takes place remains untouched.

In the case of language learning the relevant data belong to a clearly circumscribed set: the sentences of the language. When a child who is learning English hears a sentence in Chinese, it does not constitute a useful datum for constructing his grammar. The child is rarely mistaken about this. By contrast, I remember having heard, as a child, Chinese tales which are not alien to the symbolic value that the Emperor and the Nightingale have for me. The fact that a datum participates in the symbolism of one culture does not prevent its symbolic processing in a second culture. Acquisition of a symbolic mechanism appropriate for the culture in which one lives therefore does not involve treating symbolically only the materials of that culture, but rather treating materials of differing origins in a culturally-determined manner. What we may suspect is that certain materials decisively orient the construction of the symbolic mechanism and assure among the members of the same culture a relative homogeneity in this respect.

In the case of language, the set of data is defined by a state of the language at a given time and place, and no fact foreign to that state will be processed. But the corresponding notion of a state of symbolism for a given culture at a given moment does not imply any strict criterion of inclusion or exclusion. In the case of language, while each individual constructs his grammar from a sample of utterances largely different from that encountered by other subjects, the grammar he constructs is nevertheless essentially similar to that constructed by these others. Conversely, in the case of symbolism a good part of the data are similar for all the individual members of the same culture, nourished by the same myths and spectators of the same rituals. There are, however, idiosyncratic data linked to individual experience which do not belong to a shared legacy and nevertheless affect the construction of the symbolic device. The data an individual uses in learning symbolism do not constitute a sample of a fixed set similar to the sentences of a language. Such a set does not exist. By the same token, idiosyncratic data entail idiosyncrasy in the devices constructed. Symbolic devices may vary from individual to individual much more than in the case of language, even though the initial data may vary less.

Symbolism is, in large part, individual, which is doubly incomprehensible from the semiological point of view. Firstly, a system of communication works only to the extent that the underlying code is essentially the same for all; secondly, a code exhaustively defines all its messages. Symbolism, which is a non-semiological cognitive system, is not subject to these restrictions.

A corollary of this cognitive nature is that there is no multi-symbolism analogous to multi-lingualism. An individual who learns a second language internalises a second grammar, and if some interference takes place, it is on a remarkably small scale. Conversely, symbolic data, no matter what their origin, integrate themselves into a single system within a given individual.

If one could internalise several different symbolic devices, as one can learn several languages, the task of the anthropologist would thereby become considerably simpler. But the anthropologist, who little by little penetrates the symbolism of his hosts, is never able to pass from one symbolism to another as easily as he passes from one language to another. One of the first things that the anthropologist learns in the field is strictly to observe the local forms of politeness. For at least a time, he has the impression that he is acting, rather than expressing himself normally; the symbolic values of these forms of politeness escape him, or he only apprehends them upon reflection. The longer he is there, the more easily he can pass from one 'code' of politeness to another, like an actor who changes roles. But if he should become sensitive to the grace of a gesture of offering; to the nuances by which the warmth or coolness of a welcome are expressed; to the perfidiousness of a disguised insult; if at the death of a friend he comes to feel comforted, rather than troubled, by reproducing the traditional gestures of mourning; in short, if he should internalise these forms instead of imitating them: then, on returning home, he will catch himself following rules that are not in force, and resenting it when others break them.

By an effort for which he is professionally trained, the anthropologist adapts and re-adapts himself quickly enough. But an individual who has emigrated to a new society will for a long time, and perhaps forever, take as an insult, vulgarity, or delicateness what would have been such in his original milieu. By contrast, the homophonies from language to language are hardly ever misleading. One only constructs one symbolic device which experience can modify but not duplicate.

There is a moment when one can say of a child that he has learned to speak. Doubtless, he will still enrich his vocabulary, he will become better at coping with complex constructions. He has nevertheless crossed a threshold that is clearly enough delineated. Yet there is no equivalent threshold in symbolism. The external experience of daily life and the internal one of dream and reverie constantly modify schemes of symbolic interpretation. In a more dramatic way, an individual may be initiated fairly late in life to certain rites, or may convert to another religion, and thus learn a new symbolism without its following that his symbolic mechanism must have been either incomplete or radically different before. The symbolic life of an individual does not divide itself neatly into a period of learning and a period of use of an established mechanism. Symbolism, because it is cognitive, remains throughout life a learning mechanism.

Because of this, symbolism and language may evolve in very different ways. The historical evolution of language is considerably slowed down by the briefness of the learning period. Each generation can only bring a minimal contribution to this evolution, marginally modifying the conditions of learning of the following generation by changing vocabulary, approving certain 'accents', etc. Any more radical modification, for example abandoning a dialect in favour of a national language, is not, in fact, evolution of language but transformation of a social group. In the case of symbolism, on the other hand, evolution can take place not only from generation to generation, but also within one generation because the period of acquisition of symbolism is not limited to a particular chronological age. Modern societies afford a striking example of this: the characters in Balzac evoke, by means of a language very close to our own, a profoundly different symbolic universe.

Many traditional societies in which symbolism (falsely) appears to be immutable act as though they had understood the risk of too rapid an evolution; they seem to do everything to shackle it. Considerable precautions are taken to assure the identity of myths, rituals, etc. In the case of language, on the contrary, precautions may be taken to prevent the abandoning of a dialect in favour of another, but hardly to prevent its autonomous and generally unconscious evolution.

Thus, four fundamental properties contrast the data that serve in the construction of a grammar with those that serve in the construction of a symbolic mechanism.

Firstly, observable linguistic data, that is to say, phonetic data derive from auditory perception and constitute a class of distinct percepts. By contrast, symbolic data are not perceptually defined.

Secondly, linguistic data serving as the basis of the construction of a grammar are defined by belonging to a given language to the exclusion of all others. By contrast, symbolic data are not defined by belonging to a set exclusive of other sets.

Thirdly, linguistic data deriving from several languages determine, in the same individual, the construction of several grammars. By contrast, symbolic data, no matter what their source, never determine more than one symbolic mechanism in the same individual.

Fourthly, when language is learned, supplementary linguistic data interpreted by the grammar do not modify it. Language learning is soon over. By contrast, the symbolic mechanism does not process new data without itself being modified: it is not only the object of learning, but also constant learning is one of its objects.

If we take it as a cognitive system, none of these properties of symbolism is mysterious. A semiological view must either ignore them and renounce any claim to empirical validity, or take account of them and renounce any claim to internal coherence.

However, if these properties distinguish symbolism from language, they do not, still, distinguish it from the encyclopaedia. Encyclopaedic knowledge is not associated with a particular class of percepts; it is not organised in functionally equivalent and mutually exclusive systems but is integrated into a single complex mechanism in each individual; its acquisition is never over.

In what way does symbolic knowledge differ from encyclopaedic knowledge? Let us characterise the latter by contrasting it with semantic knowledge.

Semantic knowledge is about categories and not about the world. It may be expressed in the form of a set of analytic statements. For example:

(1) The lion is an animal.
(2) The unicorn is an animal.
(3) A good knife is a knife that cuts well.
(4) A single person is not married.

To know that the lion is an animal is not to know anything about lions, not even that they exist, as is shown by (2), but only something about the meaning of the word 'lion'. Similarly, anyone who knows English knows that (3) and (4) are true, even if he has never handled a knife, even if he is ignorant of all matrimonial law. We might conceive of a machine capable of correctly indicating all the paraphrases, analytic tautologies and contradictions, in short, a machine that would possess all the semantic knowledge on which a language is based, without having, for all that, the least knowledge about the world.

Encyclopaedic knowledge, conversely, is about the world. It may be expressed in the form of a set of synthetic propositions. For example:

(5) The lion is a dangerous animal.

(6) The unicorn does not exist.

(7) A good knife is expensive.

(8) Isidore is the husband of Ursula.

These statements are true or false according to the state of the world and no semantic rule determines their truth-value.

The majority of categories of thought thus include two aspects: the one, semantic, and the other, encyclopaedic. Some categories, however, have only a semantic aspect: for example, 'always' which has a sense but no referent. Conversely, proper names seem to have only an encyclopaedic aspect, but no semantic one unless we want to say that (9) is an analytic contradiction, an error about the word, and not about the thing:

(9) Ben Nevis is a man.

It is not very easy to decide where to draw the line between semantic and encyclopaedic knowledge. Examples (9) and (10)–(12) are open to discussion:

(10) The lion is a mammal.

(11) A knife has a blade and a handle.

(12) Marriage is an institution.

But the fact that there is an indefinite number of cases which, for lack of a developed semantic theory, one hesitates to take on, does not make the distinction between the semantic and the encyclopaedic any less absolute. However, without underestimating the interest of the problem, what counts here, at the level of generality at which I am operating, is not so much the position, but the existence, of the logical limit between these two types of knowledge.

Semantic knowledge about each category is finite. The semantic definition of a category or – what amounts to the same thing – the semantic component of the lexical entry that corresponds to it, specifies in a finite manner a finite

number of senses. It is possible to know everything about
the meaning of the word 'lion' or the word 'knife'. By
contrast, it is impossible to know everything about lions and
knives: encyclopaedic knowledge about such categories is
potentially infinite.

In this respect as well, symbolic knowledge resembles
encyclopaedic knowledge. It is potentially infinite too. For
example, besides the many standard metaphors that are
based on the encyclopaedic category of lion, there is a potentially indefinite number of new metaphors, dream-like associations that are no less leonine. To the very extent that
encyclopaedic knowledge is enriched, symbolic knowledge
is able to take on new knowledge and similarly enrich itself.

At first glance, symbolic knowledge is similar to encyclopaedic knowledge. Like it, it can be expressed by means of
synthetic statements. For example, for the Dorze:

(13) The leopard is a Christian animal who observes the
fasts of the Ethiopian Orthodox Church.
(14) It is taboo (*gome*) to kill a snake.
(15) Ancestor spirits feed on the blood of victims sacrificed
to them.

The truth-value of statements (13)–(15) depends, as does
that of statements (5)–(8), on the state of the world. It cannot,
in any case, be deduced from the meaning of the words used.
Even in the case of (14), which might seem dubious in this
respect, it is sufficient to observe that a Dorze may deny
that it is taboo to kill a snake just as a Christian may deny
that adultery is a sin, without this being a contradiction *in
terms*. Therefore, statement (14) is not analytic, as opposed
to (1)–(4).

In the semiological view, statements (13)–(15) need not be
taken literally. The Christianity of the leopard, for example,
should rather be understood as a kind of metaphor. Indeed
too many anthropologists have in the past tended to take

metaphors for beliefs, but it is a bit hasty to take all beliefs to be metaphors. When a Dorze states (13)–(15), for him it is not a manner of speaking; he takes it literally. He is, nevertheless, not ignorant of the art of metaphor; if he says that a valiant warrior is a lion, he doesn't imagine that he has a mane. The 'savages' themselves do not authorise us to confuse the literal and the metaphorical.

Even if literal symbolic statements and encyclopaedic statements seem to have the same form, the former are not articulated to the latter as are the latter among themselves.

Any synthetic statement implies and contradicts others. Our knowledge about the world is formed by organising statements according to these relationships, by accepting a statement only with its implications – at least the most evident ones – and similarly, by avoiding contradictions. Experience shows that encyclopaedic knowledge is not immune to incoherences and contradictions, but all practical life is based on a continuous effort to avoid or correct them.

Symbolic statements are not articulated in the same way, and similar efforts are not made with them. Not that they are incoherent among themselves, but their coherence is of another variety, and they co-exist without difficulty with encyclopaedic statements that contradict them, either directly or by implication.

A Dorze is no less careful to guard his animals on Wednesdays and Fridays, fast days, than on the other days of the week. Not because he suspects some leopards of being bad Christians, but because he takes it as true both that leopards fast and that they are always dangerous. These two statements are never compared. If an anthropologist pesters an informant about this, the latter reflects and replies: leopards don't eat meat killed on fast days, or perhaps they only eat it the next day. The problem of the long fasts that last several weeks remains to be resolved. But precisely, the informant views the question as an enigma, as a problem whose solution perforce exists, and whose premises must be correct. Leopards are dangerous every day; this he knows from experience. They are also Christians; this is guaranteed by tradition. He need not seek the solution of this paradox; he knows that there is one.

Similarly, a Christian to whom one points out a contradiction in the Gospel according to Saint Matthew, between the genealogy of Jesus who descends from Abraham and David through Joseph, and the statement which immediately follows it that Jesus is not the son of Joseph, does not for an instant dream of questioning either of the terms of the paradox and does not doubt that it is resolvable, even if the solution escapes him. By contrast, if his neighbour Jack claimed to be descended from the King of France through his father and swore at the same time that he was another man's son, he would gloat. He would not think much of the argument, dear to anthropologists, that rests on the distinction between pater and genitor. Edmund Leach invokes it in the case of Jesus (Leach 1966b: 97), but the Catholic editors of the Gospels that I have before me prefer to clarify in a footnote that the husband of Mary was also her relative. Only a miscreant would reproach Matthew for not saying this immediately. A Christian knows that there is a good reason why he does not, even if he himself does not know it. Statement (14): it is taboo to kill a snake, poses no problem if taboo is simply taken as a social rule. Encyclopaedic knowledge is not only about brute facts, but also about institutional facts. A statement such as:

(16) Adultery is a crime.

is true or false according to the text of the law.
By contrast:

(17) Adultery is a sin.

is a statement that, even if it is written in the law of the church, is not about an institutional fact, but about a brute fact. In stating that adultery is a sin, the theologian – unlike the legislator or the jurist uttering (16) – is not making a decision or referring to a human decision, but affirms the existence of a state of things that it is not for humans to modify. He may certainly change his interpretation, but not bring into question the existence of what he is interpreting.

There are simple empirical criteria for deciding on the truth of (16): it is sufficient to consult the law code which itself is normative and therefore neither true nor false. There are also empirical criteria for deciding that:

(18) Adultery is pleasant.

By contrast, there is no empirical criterion for deciding on the truth of (17). No knowledge arising from experience will ever refute the 'fact' that adultery is a sin. (17) can only be contradicted by equally irrefutable statements.

In appearance, statement (14) (the Dorze taboo) is subject to empirical falsification. In theory, indeed, the transgression of a taboo causes the misfortune of the guilty one. The correlation or non-correlation between the two facts is perfectly observable, even if the causal nature of the link is more speculative. To explain why new taboos are observed, or old ones have fallen into desuetude, the Dorze use experimental arguments: those who have transgressed the former have suffered; those who transgressed the latter remained unaffected.

However, a Dorze who believes all this quite consistently relates transgression to misfortune in the reverse order to the theoretical one. A misfortune occurs: a member of the family falls ill, a cow dies, there is a poor harvest. The family head consults the diviner, who says, for example: 'Taboo of impurity, taboo of the snake.' He proposes several solutions. The consultant remembers, 'Oh, yes, I threw a stone at a snake', or 'The dog got out through the stable drain-hole', etc. There are always transgressions in reserve. If a Dorze generally avoids them, he commits them, occasionally, without great disquiet. He takes it that there are times when it is more dangerous to leave a snake alive than to kill it. Once the taboo is transgressed, he does not generally worry about expiating immediately. Instead he will wait for the time when, on the occasion of a misfortune, a diviner will evoke the category of taboos to which this transgression belongs. The consultant will then point to it as a cause whose precise effects he had not until then speculated upon. In other words, causal reasoning is always *a posteriori*.

An illustration: my friend Wondimu has his father sacrifice a sheep for him. The carcass is cut up, and the entrails are taken out carefully, so as not to tear the mesenteric membrane before the diviner has had a chance at it. The chosen diviner is late, his son is there. This son examines the entrails and discovers a taboo of the snake. We leave to go and meet the diviner. On the way, Wondimu admits to me that several months before he had killed a snake, and marvels at the clairvoyance of the diviner's son: a further sacrifice seems absolutely to be required. We finally find the diviner, we sit down, and we consult him. The diviner reveals several benign taboos, but not that of the snake. Wondimu makes no further mention of it. Rather, he seems relieved – it will wait for another occasion.

The empirical proof evoked by the Dorze to justify his statements about taboos is therefore fictitious: it is the diviner and his client who decide which transgression to associate with which misfortune and which taboo to verify 'experimentally'. For them, the proof is conclusive and bears witness to a state of the world and not to a decision. But this knowledge of taboos, like Christian knowledge about sin, is immune to all empirical falsification while encyclopaedic knowledge is subject to it. In other words, statements about taboo are not articulated with statements about the world as the latter are articulated among themselves, and this not only in the logic of the anthropologist, but in that of the Dorze themselves.

Statement (13) about leopards could easily be put to empirical proof, but the Dorze do not pay any heed. Conversely, statement (14) about the taboo of the snake is unfalsifiable and the Dorze comment on it willingly in experimental terms which are not pertinent. Statement (15) is in this respect midway between (13) and (14). It implies on the one hand that the blood of sacrificed animals must be absorbed and therefore must disappear, which is readily verifiable; on the other hand, it presupposes the existence of particular entities, ancestor spirits, and this presupposition is immune, in the encyclopaedic knowledge of the Dorze, to any chance of empirical falsification. At one and the same time, a whole series of anecdotes is proposed which support the existence of spirits. As regards the paradox of the blood which is consumed but still there, they are content to admit that it is resolvable. That is enough, at least as long as symbolic knowledge is not articulated with encyclopaedic knowledge.

To observe this lack of articulation shifts but does not resolve the problem. A certain mode of organisation of knowledge does not operate in the case of symbolism. The inanity of symbolic statements derives not from a random set of faulty reasonings, but from a systematic relaxation of constraints. A good number of symbolic utterances are presented not as figurative, but as literally true, and it is not enough to describe their characteristic illogicality; rather, it must be explained. We must say what this knowledge, which is neither semantic nor encyclopaedic, is about.

The paradox of symbolism becomes clearer if it is formulated as follows: under what conditions is it logically possible to hold a synthetic statement to be true without comparing it with other synthetic statements which are susceptible of validating or invalidating it? Put in this way, the paradox is easy enough to resolve. Take a statement p. If p is part of my encyclopaedic knowledge just as are other statements, it is necessarily compared with them. But it may figure in another manner, as part of statement (19):

(19) 'p' is true.

It is perfectly possible to know (19) without knowing p. If, for example, someone gives me a sealed envelope that contains a page on which is written the statement p, while telling me that p is true, I will know (19), but I will still not know p. Or, to take another example: of the two statements (20) and (21), only the second is part of my encyclopaedic knowledge:

(20) $e = mc^2$.
(21) '$e = mc^2$' is valid.

Statement (21) is directly part of my encyclopaedia and it is quite rationally that I take it to be true. (21) seems true to me because from experience I take the sources of (20) to be reliable. By contrast, (20) is not directly part of my encyclopaedia. Not being a physicist, I am incapable of giving (20) a precise import, of validating it or invalidating it by means of other synthetic statements. (20) figures in my encyclopaedia only as part of (21) and only in quotes.

Imagine now that in the encyclopaedia of a Dorze there were not, as it seemed, statements (13)–(15), but rather statements (22)–(24):

(22) '(13)' is true.
(23) '(14)' is true.
(24) '(15)' is true.

The empirical considerations that would have had to lead imperatively to rejecting (13) and (15), to wit, that cattle are eaten every day by leopards and that the blood of the sacrifice is never absorbed, do not have the same force against (22) and (24). There are indeed two possibilities: these considerations show either that (22) and (24) are false or else that (13) and (15) must be differently interpreted as to their implications. Similarly, the impossibility of proving as facts the efficacy of taboos and the existence of ancestors, which – by virtue of the principle of parsimony that governs encyclopaedic knowledge – causes us to reject (14) and (15), does not have the same force against (23) and (24). Faced with (22)–(24), a Dorze must think either that the elders say the first thing that comes into their heads, or else that there are statements whose empirical import he is incapable of understanding, and whose truth-value he is incapable of establishing, and that (13)–(15) are statements of this sort. In other words, if we wish to preserve for the word 'statement' the precise sense given it by logicians, that is to say, if statements are conceptual representations analysed in full, without ambiguity, and having a truth-value, we should say (13)–(15) are not statements, but conceptual representations only partly analysed, of which one does not know for certain whether they express a statement, and if so, which. Empirical arguments are not lacking that would permit a Dorze to prefer the second hypothesis. Moreover, every child has learned the truth of certain utterances long before understanding their import.

As I write this book, the intricate ideas of Dr Lacan are fashionable. Many take to be true:

(25) 'The unconscious is structured like a language.'

A critical reader tries to see which statement is expressed by utterance (25) so as to evaluate its truth. The structure of language being a part of the structure of the unconscious, he asks himself if the part is here a model of the whole, if the general properties of language extend to all the unconscious, if the unconscious is a code, or is made up of codes, etc. For my part, I am incapable of conceiving a true statement that would conform to the sense of (25). I doubt, however, that a Lacanian would yield to my arguments. If we ask him the precise import of (25), even though incapable of defining it, he will not doubt its truth. The problem, for him, is not to validate or invalidate a statement. He knows that (25) expresses a valid statement, but he does not know which one. Thus, he searches. Doing so, his mind opens itself to a whole series of problems, certain possibilities appear, certain relationships impose themselves. He has therefore not necessarily wasted his time in taking utterance (26) as valid. By taking it in quotes, he opens it to interpretation, he treats it symbolically. We could give more examples and show that for many Marxists, Freudians or structuralists, their doctrine functions symbolically. They take its theses to be true without knowing exactly what they imply. Empirical counterarguments, in so far as they concern themselves with them, lead them not to reject these theses, but to modify their import. More generally, in our society a large number of symbolic statements are of the form of (26) where science plays the role of the ancestors:

(26) 'p' is scientific.

So-called symbolic statements figure in encyclopaedic knowledge not directly, but obliquely by conceptual representations in quotes, in contexts of the type '"p" is true'. This is not just a way of dealing with the problem of the apparent irrationality of symbolism. If we accept this point of view, a certain number of properties of symbolism become clear and contribute to motivating it, independently of the particular paradox that in the first instance led to its adoption.

Research on symbolism has come up against two major difficulties: how to treat together cultural and individual symbolism? How to treat together symbolism given as truthful, and symbolism given as figurative? A first approach consists in not treating them together at all and in considering that the intersection of these two distinctions defines four independent groups of facts. This solution is scarcely satisfying. It is counter-intuitive, and leaves unexplained the homogeneity of form and content among these four groups of facts. Another approach consists in reducing one type of data to another: for example, the Freudians generally reduce the cultural to the individual, which Leach (1958) has aptly criticised. But he leaves himself open to a similar criticism by tending to reduce beliefs to figures of speech. No view of symbolism is satisfactory if it makes these distinctions absolute, or if it obliterates them.

The contrast between cultural and individual symbolism only raises difficulties from a semiological point of view; from a cognitive point of view, the problem is not very different from that of the encyclopaedia. The more specific problem posed by the contrast between beliefs and figures of speech may be dealt with without giving up either what relates them or what distinguishes them.

First, a word about the notion of belief. Rodney Needham (1972) has shown convincingly the conceptual confusion which surrounds the use of this notion. The notion of belief, like that of the symbol, is neither universal nor homogeneous within our culture. The notion of the symbol is linked to a view of symbolism which I take to be false, so that I hesitate to use it, even with a technical definition, for fear that it will retain, in spite of this, all its misleading connotations. It seems to me that the notion of belief has neither suffered nor benefited from a similar elaboration, except among theologians. It is therefore possible to utilise it, giving it a technical sense whose extension covers at least some of its usual uses. I shall call belief a conceptual representation p that only figures in the encyclopaedia of an individual as part of a statement of the form ' "p" is true'.

Now consider figurative conceptual representations such as:

(27) The lion is king of the animals.
(28) A rolling stone gathers no moss.
(29) Your feet are dreaming of colours.

Representations (27)–(29) have no place in the knowledge of an individual except in quotes and in contexts such as:

(30) '(27)' is a manner of speaking.
(31) '(28)' is a proverb used on such and such occasions.
(32) '(29)' is an advertising slogan for socks.

(27) and (29) are semantic anomalies. In (27) 'the lion' designates a species, while 'the king' designates an individual; in (29) 'your feet' could not be the subject of 'dream' for 'dream' only admits as subjects thinking beings. Thus, (27) and (29) lack truth-value and cannot be entered directly into the encyclopaedia. (28), on the other hand, makes an admissible encyclopaedic statement. But it would only be of interest to botanists and pedologists who would have no use for its archaic formulation. In the shared encyclopaedia of the English (28) figures only in quotes and as a proverb.

The particular contexts in which these conceptual representations occur here matter little; what matters is their principle. First, figurative expressions only enter into encyclopaedic knowledge in quotes and accompanied by a commentary that clarifies the nature and perhaps the conditions of use of the expression. Next, these commentaries are open to a certain amount of cultural or individual idiosyncrasy. Notions such as 'saying', 'proverb', 'slogan', and even 'metaphor', 'allegory', 'symbol' are not universal but cultural. Within the same culture, not everyone gives them the same extension. But universally, figurative symbolic representations are learned, memorised and produced in quotes, and in a context that lays them open to interpretation by preventing their literal acceptance. In other words, they enter in the general form:

(33) 'p' is a figure,

even if each culture, and to a lesser extent each individual, realises and diversifies this general form differently.

To say that figurative utterances are represented in quotes is, by the way, only to formulate in new and more explicit terms the old rhetorical view revived by Roman Jakobson (1960), a view that Todorov explains in this way: 'Figures might be nothing more than *language perceived as such*; in other words, a use of language in which the latter ceases more or less to fulfil its semantic function...and takes on an opaque existence' (Ducrot and Todorov 1972: 351–2).

The first advantage of the formulation I am proposing is to make manifest the shared properties of beliefs and figures, and thus to resolve one of the classic problems of the study of symbolism. This formulation has, besides, other useful consequences.

Representation in quotes of the figure is accompanied by commentaries varying according to cultures and individuals. The same is true for representation in quotes of belief. Even if we accept that truth is a universal category of thought, the notions that express it in different languages are different and diversified. In Dorze, for example, the word *adhe* designates both conformity to facts and conformity to tradition. The word *ts'ilo* designates both he who reports faithfully what he has seen or heard, and he who speaks and acts conforming to tradition and to his own commitments. This lexical fusion in no way implies that in the exercise of their thought, the Dorze do not distinguish the empirical truth from reported speech. When a Dorze says of a statement that it is *adhe*, he does not mean to say on one occasion that it is true in our sense, and on another, that it is traditional; it is true in all cases, and its truth guaranteed either by experience or by tradition, that is to say, by the non-reproducible experience of the ancestors.

Unlike the underlying universal category, the concept of truth not only varies from culture to culture, but also may be diversified within the same culture. Thus, in our culture the forms (26) and (34)–(36) may function as particular cases of the general form of belief:

(34) '*p*' is a revealed truth.
(35) Lacan knows that '*p*'.
(36) '*p*' is Marxist.

Notation in quotes for conceptual representations of beliefs or figures indicates what they have in common; they are not entirely analysed into propositions nor fully compared with encyclopaedic statements. I shall clarify the nature of this blockage and later I shall show how it entails a specifically symbolic treatment. The proposed formulation underscores at the same time the difference between belief and figure; this difference does not relate to internal properties of conceptual representations in quotes, but to the encyclopaedic commentary that accompanies these representations. In this commentary, the figure is explicitly given as such; by contrast, the belief is given as a true statement, that is to say, as an ordinary encyclopaedic statement. This difference expresses an evident intuition, to wit, that the symbolicity of figures is explicit or implicit, while beliefs are consciously considered as being part of ordinary encyclopaedic knowledge and therefore are only unconsciously symbolic.

When the symbolic character of a belief reaches the level of consciousness, its status as belief is modified. In the limiting case a belief may become a figure, and vice versa, without changing its form. Only the encyclopaedic commentary, and with it the conscious status, will necessarily be altered.

This distinction between a stable representation in quotes and a changing encyclopaedic commentary helps us to understand the fact that, between belief and figure, intermediate states or even indetermination can be observed. A Christian, for example, may hesitate between a literal interpretation and a figurative one of the Eucharist, miracles, etc. If p is a statement in the Gospels, it is not necessary that the Christian take 'p' to be true. It suffices that:

(37) ' "p" is the word of God ' is true.

As Pascal says, 'When the word of God, which is true, is literally false, it is spiritually true' (Pascal, *Pensées*: 687). In other words, God may speak figuratively and we may put an utterance in quotes in the encyclopaedia without clarifying whether it should be understood as a literal truth or as a figurative one. Generally speaking, a whole part of theological debate bears not on representations in quotes, but on the encyclopaedic commentary which is appropriate to them.

It will have been noted that in example (37), the commentary of the representation in quotes is itself in quotes. In other words, a symbolic conceptual representation may itself be embedded in another symbolic representation. The proposed formulation permits the integration of the suggestion made in Chapter 2 according to which the exegesis of a symbol is itself symbolic, and constitutes a development, not an interpretation, of what it is supposed to explain. Take again the case of the Ndembu *museng'u*, which is the object of three conceptual representations:

(38) The *museng'u* brings success in hunting.
(39) The *museng'u* signifies multiplicity.
(40) The *museng'u* bears many fruits.

These representations are articulated among themselves: (40) justifies (39), and (39) justifies (38). But, as we have seen, these justifications are not based on any generalisation that the Ndembu would accept as true outside a ritual context. They are invalid in their form, and non-verifiable in their conclusions. These justifications are symbolic, they appear in quotes, and are articulated for example in the following way:

(41) ' "(38)" is true because ' "(39)" is true because "(40)" ' '
  is true.

So far, three arguments militate in favour of the putting of symbolic knowledge into quotes in the encyclopaedia: Firstly, the problem of the irrationality of beliefs in general is, if not resolved, at least circumscribed. Secondly, the similarities and differences between beliefs and figures are clarified. Thirdly, the fact that the symbolic commentary becomes part of symbolism itself may thus be explicated.

The putting in quotes of symbolic knowledge has the further advantage of clearly contrasting it with semantic knowledge on the one hand, and with the rest of encyclopaedic knowledge on the other; we have already noted the originality of Lévi-Strauss who, unlike his predecessors – or in any case much more clearly than any of them – elaborated the hypothesis of a symbolic knowledge that was about categories and not about the world. If it were about the world, symbolic discourse would be inadmissible and one would have to see those that hold it both as virtuosos in imagination and defectives in reason. On the other hand, the idea of a symbolic discourse that would be properly about semantic categories comes up against two objections: Firstly, as has been noted, it is not analytic. Secondly, as Lévi-Strauss notes, the knowledge of the world is not absent from it, but, unlike synthetic discourse, it constitutes within it a means and not an end. A correct view, but a somewhat obscure one that the proposed formulation will now, I hope, allow us to elucidate.

In the memory two entries correspond to each category of knowledge. The first entry, a semantic one, determines the analytic relationships that the category has with others. The second entry, an encyclopaedic one, enumerates the knowledge that bears on the categorised object. The knowledge that the dog and the fox are animals is semantic and is specified by the first entry. The knowledge that the dog is domestic, the fox wild, that one is used to hunt the other, is encyclopaedic and is specified in the second entry. This distinction made, it is clear that the symbolic value of a category relates essentially to the encyclopaedic entry.

The symbolic value of 'fox' owes nothing to the sense of the word, and everything to what we know or believe about foxes: to their skill as predators, their look, their coat, etc. What matters, symbolically speaking, is neither how foxes are semantically defined nor what foxes actually are, but what is known of them, what is said of them, what is believed about them. The example of the dog in this last respect is absolutely clear. In expressions like 'a dog's life', 'a filthy dog', 'to treat like a dog', the symbolic weight has little to do with the actual canine condition. But these expressions figure in quotes in the encyclopaedic entry 'dog'. If one says 'cunning as a fox', an expression which, unlike the preceding ones, perhaps corresponds to reality, what happens here is that a normal encyclopaedic statement is put in quotes and serves no longer to express knowledge about foxes but something else by means of that knowledge. In other words, symbolic knowledge is neither about semantically understood categories, nor about the world, but about the encyclopaedic entries of categories. This knowledge is neither about words nor about things, but about the memory of words and things. It is a knowledge about knowledge, a meta-encyclopaedia in the encyclopaedia and not – contrary to the semiological view – a meta-language in language.

To say that symbolic representations are in quotes is to say further that symbolic knowledge is not about the object of these representations but, on the contrary, has these representations as its object. Whence comes the possibility of formulating more usefully – if not that of resolving – another problem encountered in approaches to symbolism. Some utterances are clearly and absolutely symbolic: liturgical formulae, invocations, myths, figurative idioms, etc., either because they have no other interpretation than their symbolic one, or else because all other interpretations are absurd. We might therefore be tempted to define symbolism by what these utterances have in common either in their form or their content and by what opposes them to non-symbolic utterances. But there is no non-symbolic utterance which is not capable, in some conditions, of becoming symbolic. It takes only, for example, recognition in the utterances:

(42) No entry,
(43) Keep left,
(44) She never misses a trick in the pub,

respectively of a sexual allusion, a political allusion, and a Spoonerism, to give them a symbolic value that they do not normally have.

It is thus anyhow impossible to define symbolic knowledge in terms of the properties of the objects or of the utterances conceptually represented. We might then be reduced to saying that what is symbolic is that which is treated as such and that certain objects, and in particular, certain utterances, are always treated as symbolic, while others may be, but need not be.

Yet, if symbolic knowledge is about conceptual representations, we readily see: Firstly, that all encyclopaedic statements about an object in the world may themselves be objects of a symbolic knowledge and may be put in quotes. Secondly, that a conceptual representation that is not articulated to the encyclopaedia, i.e., that is not an independent statement in it, may nevertheless figure in it in quotes and only in quotes – that is to say, as the object of an exclusively symbolic knowledge. We see besides that the readjustments of encyclopaedic knowledge (for example the discovery that it is not Santa Claus but Mother who puts the presents in the stockings, or else that behind the masks it is not the ancestor who is hiding, but Daddy) entail not necessarily the rejection of a conceptual representation but alternatively, putting it in quotes.

Before clarifying and illustrating this view, I must do justice to an apparent objection. In the preceding chapters, I have implicitly accepted that symbolism was ritual as well as verbal, and many of my illustrations were of the first sort. Now, I am characterising symbolism in terms of the logical status of statements.

An utterance, a text, may express statements and be put in quotes. By contrast, to return to an example I have made much use of, to put butter in quotes won't even make a sandwich. Is this to say that from now on I reduce symbolism to the verbal and deprive myself of the means of dealing with gestures and objects which up to this point I have considered to be part of symbolism?

No. The statements I am talking about are not those that are uttered; they are those that the mind of a subject constructs by means of what he hears uttered, and also by means of what he senses, what he sees, what he touches, and the sounds he hears which are not speech. Knowledge, even if it is transmitted in speech, does not reproduce that speech but reconstructs its propositional content while modifying and supplementing it. Even if it concerns non-verbal experience, knowledge is constructed in a set of statements which need only be made conscious for speech to be able to transmit them. It is these underlying statements that are or are not the object of a logical calculus, that are or are not in quotes.

As an example, take mime. The mime says nothing. Armed with a net, he chases a butterfly. He holds his breath, tiptoes forward, stops, waves his net briskly. Missed! He follows the butterfly with his eyes, approaches it again, and this time catches it. Between thumb and forefinger, he delicately takes the insect, which struggles. There is no net, there is no butterfly, the mime's look is directed at nothing and his fingers close on emptiness. What then is this description of a butterfly chase that the spectator has mentally constructed? A set of statements in quotes.

To take another example: the sacrificer. The sacrificer talks to his ancestors. He takes a sheep, strokes its back three times, throws it to the ground on its right side, slits its throat, wets his hand in its blood and sprinkles it before him so that the ancestors will consume it. No ancestor is present, neither to hear the sacrificer, nor to observe the correctness of his gestures, nor to drink the blood. Yet the spectators have witnessed not just any slaughtering of just any sheep, but a sacrificial giving. They know that the whispered words of the sacrificer have been heard, that the blood, which still hasn't dried, has been consumed by the ancestors. What then is this description of a sacrifice that the spectators have mentally constructed? A set of statements in quotes.

The difference? The spectators of the mime know perfectly well that the mental representation they have constructed does not correspond to reality. Contrarily, the participants in the sacrifice take it to be effective. To put it another way, just as with a figure, but without a word having been spoken, the mime's representation participates in a conscious symbolism. Just as with belief, and even if the invocations that accompany it remain incomprehensible, the representation of the sacrifice participates in an unconscious symbolism. In the one case as in the other, the representation is in quotes, open to interpretation.

Symbolicity is therefore not a property either of objects, or of acts, or of utterances, but of conceptual representations that describe or interpret them. Theoretical approaches that would look in objects, acts or utterances for the properties constitutive of symbolism must be bound to fail. By contrast, an adequate theory of symbolism will describe the properties which a conceptual representation must possess to be the object of a putting in quotes and of a symbolic treatment. We can now be more specific.

When information holds the conceptual attention, whether it impinges on it or whether it is sought after, two conditions must be fulfilled for it to undergo a calculus of validation: Firstly, it must be described by entirely analysed statements without which no logical calculus is possible. Secondly, the previous knowledge that this information may enrich or directly modify – that is to say, the encyclopaedic knowledge that is about the same objects – must be mobilised, without which the calculus of validation, which operates by comparing the implications of the new statements with the statements previously validated, cannot be accomplished.

A conceptual representation therefore comprises two sets of statements: focal statements, which describe the new information, and auxiliary statements which link the new information to the encyclopaedic memory. If the one set fails to describe, and the other set fails to link, the new information cannot be integrated into acquired knowledge.

When a conceptual representation has thus failed to make new information assimilable by the memory, either, because of an insufficient analysis of the information itself, or else because of an insufficient mobilisation of acquired knowledge, it would seem that the information can only be rejected.

However, a new object has been created: the conceptual representation itself, a possible object of a second representation. I clarify my hypothesis: the conceptual mechanism never works in vain; when a conceptual representation fails to establish the relevance of its object, it becomes itself the object of a second representation. This second representation is not constructed by the conceptual mechanism which turned out to be powerless, but by the symbolic mechanism that then takes over. The symbolic mechanism tries to establish by its own means the relevance of the defective conceptual representation.

To return to Lévi-Strauss' image, the symbolic mechanism is the *bricoleur* of the mind. It starts from the principle that waste-products of the conceptual industry deserve to be saved because something can always be made of them. But the symbolic mechanism does not try to decode the information it processes. It is precisely because this information has partly escaped the conceptual code, the most powerful of the codes available to humans, that it is, in the final analysis, submitted to it. It is therefore not a question of discovering the meaning of symbolic representations but, on the contrary, of inventing a relevance and a place in the memory for them despite the failure in this respect of the conceptual categories of meaning. A representation is symbolic precisely to the extent that it is not entirely explicable, that is to say, expressible by semantic means. Semiological views are therefore not merely inadequate; they hide, from the outset, the defining features of symbolism.

5

The Symbolic Mechanism

Smells. The conceptual representation of smells is too much of a special case and too poorly studied to confirm the cognitive view of symbolism; however, it provides a very good illustration and suggests several lines of development.

Smells have two noteworthy properties, one to do with the way they are conceptualised, and the other with their place in the memory.

Even though the human sense of smell can distinguish hundreds of thousands of smells and in this regard is comparable to sight or hearing, in none of the world's languages does there seem to be a classification of smells comparable, for example, to colour classification. Ethno-linguists systematically describe colour classifications, often containing several hundred terms ordered under a small number of basic categories (and which are probably universal – see Berlin and Kay 1969 and Conklin's discussion [Conklin 1973]). We would search in vain for a similar work on smells; perhaps this is a sign of lack of imagination on the part of scholars, but more likely it is because there is nothing for such a work to be about.

Certainly, terms and expressions are not lacking to designate smells, but they almost always do so in terms of their causes or their effects. Their cause: the smell of incense, the smell of a rose, the smell of coffee, the smell of wet grass, a putrid smell, an animal smell, etc.; their effects: a nauseating smell, a heady perfume, an appetising smell. While in the domain of colours, similar designations end up by becoming lexicalised and losing all metonymic character ('rose', 'orange', and 'purple' may be used without evoking respectively the flower, fruit and dye), in the domain of smells, on the contrary, metonymy remains active and infallibly evokes cause or effect. In the domain of colours, the terms are hierarchically organised (vermilion being a sub-category of red; indigo of blue, etc.), and linked among themselves by relations of compatibility or of incompatibility (blue-green being possible, but not blue-yellow, etc.). In the domain of smells, there is nothing similar; the only possible classification is that of their causes. Thus, true enough, the smell of a lion is an animal smell but this derives from a classification of animals and not from a non-existent taxonomy of smells.

There is no semantic field of smells. The notion of smells only has as lexical sub-categories general terms such as 'stench' and 'perfume'. Our knowledge about different smells figures in the encyclopaedia not in an autonomous domain, but scattered among all the categories whose referents have olfactive qualities.

Whence, probably, comes the particular behaviour of smells in the memory. Generally, memorised information may be retrieved in two ways: either by recognition – when in the presence of new information, one remembers that one already has it; or else by recall – that is to say, independent of an external stimulus. Everything one is really capable of recalling, one is *a fortiori* capable of recognising. For example, with nothing apple-green before me, I can mentally invoke an apple-green surface, and when I actually see one, I have no hesitation at all in identifying it. Certain types of information are easier to recognise than to recall in the absence of an external stimulus. Each of us is capable of recognising hundreds or thousands of faces but can only recall a very few among them. Smells are an extreme case in this respect: one recognises them, but one doesn't recall them. If I wish to recall the smell of a rose, it is in fact a visual image that I invoke; a bouquet of roses under my nose; and in the same way I will recall a church that smelled of incense, a pillow that kept the scent of patchouli, and I will almost have the impression that I sense that scent – a misleading impression, however, which will fade as soon as, relinquishing the recollection of the object it emanated from, I try mentally to reconstitute the scent itself.

If olfactive memory fails in the area of direct remembrance (except, perhaps, for a few exceptionally gifted or trained individuals), its efficaciousness in the area of recognition is exceptional. One can, at a distance of years, recognise a smell one has only smelled once, and know first of all that one has smelled it before, then – like a magician who plucks a long multi-coloured string of handkerchiefs out of a top hat that seemed empty – one can recover by means of that recognition a whole series of memories that one didn't know one still had.

I believe we must relate the absence of a semantic field of smells, the impossibility of directly invoking recollection of them, and their extraordinary evocative power. When a smell impinges on the conceptual attention without the latter being able to represent it by an analysed description, the mind is as it were brought to a standstill by this failure, which it then turns into a success of a different order. Unable to find the means for describing this information in its stock of acquired knowledge, it abandons the search for the missing concept in favour of a symbolic commentary on its absence, by constructing or reconstructing not a representation of the object, but a representation of that representation. Thus, the smell only holds the attention in order to re-orient it towards what surrounds it.

Some may be surprised that I stress the conceptual representation of smells as belonging to the field of symbolism – be it only under certain conditions. They belong, however, by virtue of the accepted definitions according to which the symbol is the part for the whole, or the object that gives rise to thoughts of something other than itself, or the motivated sign, etc. Smells should be symbols *par excellence*. So much so that it should be surprising not that I include smells as part of symbolism, but that others have neglected to do so. On reflection, this omission is easily enough explained: it has to do with the difficulty semiologists have in recognising the symbolic nature of natural phenomena whose psychological effects it is all too clearly an abuse to describe in terms of a code. True, they recognise the symbolic accord between a storm and anger, between the full moon and declarations of love, etc., but only to the extent that this accord is the object of an institutionalised cultural representation. Certain smells, such as that of incense, are institutionalised and belong in this respect to what semiologists call a cultural code. But it is in the area of individual symbolism, in their ability to evoke recollections and sentiments that are withheld from social communication, that these olfactive impressions take on all their force. Also, this neglect on the part of semiologists of the sense of smell is only a special case of their inability to account for those symbolic phenomena which bypass all forms of coded communication and set up direct links between nature observed and the inward state of the observer. As though the 'sense of nature' only produced the symbolic by means of the works of poets in which one studied it; as though, in this respect, each of us were not his own poet!

The example of smells suggests and illustrates several important points:
– Firstly, it confirms the independence of symbolism from verbalisation and its dependence on conceptualisation.
– Secondly, it shows that putting in quotes depends on the subject's ability to mobilise on the one hand the means of analysis – that is to say, the semantic definition of concepts –

and on the other, the means of validation – that is to say, the encyclopaedic characterisation of concepts.

– Thirdly, it shows that this ability to mobilise is affected both by constant factors and by variable ones. The non-existence of a taxonomy of smells is, in this respect, a constant factor. The ease of recognition of a particular stimulus is a variable factor.

– Fourthly, it shows that the factors that vary may do so according to the culture, according to the individual, and according to the particular situation of the moment: olfactive education varies with cultures and individuals; the register of immediately recognisable smells varies from individual to individual and according to the period of their lives; attention to olfactive stimuli varies with the momentary situation. All these factors, constant or variable, determine the conceptual means mobilised in a particular situation and, therefore, the individual's skill in making the conceptual representation correspond to the information that holds his attention. When this information exceeds his means of conceptualisation, the conceptual representation itself will be incomplete – either from the point of view of analysability, or from the point of view of relevance – and it will be put in quotes.

The example of smells also gives an intuitive glimpse of symbolic processing itself, and not only of the initial conditions for putting in quotes. Symbolic processing appears to have two aspects: one, a displacement of attention, or *focalisation;* and the other, a search in the memory, or *evocation.*

In order to understand these two aspects, we must return to the conditions in which conceptual representations are set up.

At a given moment, the information memorised by an

individual is divided into two parts: the one is mobilised by his intellectual activity and constitutes active, working memory; the other, much larger, plays no part in this activity and constitutes passive, long-term memory. Information in the active memory, if it remains unused, returns to the passive memory or else disappears at the end of several hours. Information stored in the passive memory may, on the contrary, stay there indefinitely.

New information is presented. For example, I hear the name of someone I know. The information stored in the passive memory which directly concerns this person – in short, the contents of the encyclopaedic entry that I have set up for him – transfers, at least in part, from the passive memory to the active memory. New information thus mobilises the encyclopaedic knowledge directly relating to the concepts that describe it.

The intellect now has to relate the representation of the new information to the active memory – that is, to make the new information assimilable to the active memory so that it may ultimately, if need be, be stored in the passive memory.

A conceptual representation therefore takes a form which might be visualised as conical: at the top, the statements that describe the new information and focus the attention. At the base, the active memory. Between the two, the auxiliary statements that may be deduced from the conjunction of the focal and memorised statements. These auxiliary statements relate the new information to the active memory and allow the one to be integrated into the other.

It may be, however, that the working of the conceptual mechanism fails to make the new information relevant in this way. For example – and this is what takes place in the case of smells – the new information may have been only insufficiently analysed so that the active memory has not been supplemented by the mobilisation of additional encyclopaedic entries. Or else – and we shall see examples of this – the auxiliary statements that would establish the relevance of the new information cannot be deduced from those contained in the active memory, or even enter into contradiction with them. In either case, one of the necessary conditions for the new information to be integrated into the memory has not been satisfied and the working of the conceptual mechanism is aborted. What then remains is an inassimilable conceptual representation which is put in quotes to make it the object of a second representation, this time a symbolic one.

Given this, I shall go on to clarify my hypotheses on focalisation and on evocation. Firstly, the focus of attention moves from the statements at the 'top of the cone' to the unfulfilled conceptual conditions. Thus in the case of smells, the attention moves from the olfactive stimulus to the fact that, having thought one recognised it, one finds that the memory necessary for its identification is lacking.

Secondly, this unfulfilled condition itself becomes the top of a cone the base of which, this time, is in the passive memory. This base is a field whose limits vary and which contains all the information by means of which the unfulfilled condition may be re-evaluated and, possibly, fulfilled. Evocation consists in passing in review and in testing the information contained in this field.

For example, in the case of smells, the evocational field comprises all recollections likely to corroborate the feeling of recognition, and it is these recollections that evocation passes in review. Whereas the use of a concept in a conceptual representation allows the direct invoking to the encyclopaedic entry that it subsumes, the putting in quotes of a representation and the accompanying focalisation allow the delimitation of a field in which the required information is likely to be found. Symbolism thus provides a second mode of access to the memory: evocation, appropriate when invocation fails.

In the terms of modern cognitive psychology, the failure of a sequential process triggers a parallel process, thus inverting the normal order of cognitive processes (see, for example, Neisser 1967).

It is essential to understand that a symbolic representation determines a focal condition, determines an evocational field, but does not determine the paths of evocation. The focal condition is the very one which, by remaining unfulfilled, has led to the putting in quotes of the representation. The evocational field includes all information susceptible of fulfilling the focal condition. But evocation may revive information that turns out to be more interesting, better able to capture the attention than the representation in quotes or the focal condition itself. For example, in trying to identify a smell, one may revive memories that are more captivating than the smell itself, more insistent than the original desire one had to identify it. This relative freedom of evocation is at the very basis of the social use of this psychological mechanism, symbolism.

As a metaphorical illustration of these hypotheses, consider a student in a library. He has before him a certain number of books: the active memory. The vast majority of books, which are still on the shelves, are the passive memory. When, in the course of his work, he comes across a reference which interests him, he may, by using the card catalogue, immediately find the book he needs. But it may also happen that he wants further information on a subject he has not entirely defined, and does not know which volume to consult. The only option is to search through the shelves on which the relevant works might be found. Often, he stops to thumb through books that at the outset he had no need of. And, just as any library user acquires at length a dual knowledge of the stacks, on the one hand by consulting the card catalogue and on the other, by scanning the shelves in a more and more confident manner, so, aside from the direct invocation of encyclopaedic knowledge which is the job of the conceptual mechanism, the symbolic mechanism creates its own pathways in the memory, these evocations which anything may set in motion and nothing seems able to stop.

We have, then, a triad: the putting in quotes of a defective conceptual representation – focalisation on the underlying condition responsible for the initial defect – and evocation in a field of the memory delimited by the focalisation. This triad characterises not only the symbolism of smells, but symbolism in general as well. Only the initial representations, the unfulfilled conditions, the location and breadth of the evocational field vary. One of the tasks of theoretical research on symbolism is that of characterising these properties more clearly. Let us note in passing that there is a relationship between these properties, or at least the two last-mentioned, and the Freudian notions of displacement and of condensation: to a certain extent, focalisation corresponds to Freudian displacement; evocation corresponds to condensation; but the process is considered here not from the point of view of symbolic production, but from the reverse point of view, that of interpretation. I shall not elaborate on this parallel whose limitations are obvious, and I shall do little to clarify these hypotheses; I shall merely illustrate them briefly.

Irony. Compare utterances (1) and (2) (*The Parisian* being an imaginary daily known to be devoted to sensationalism).

(1) Jerome buys *The Parisian* even though he is not interested in sensationalism!
(2) Arthur buys *The Parisian* even though he doesn't need lavatory paper!

The conceptual representation of these utterances must contain a *sous-entendu* that accounts for the 'even though'.

For example, the *sous-entendu* (3) for (1) and (4) for (2):

(3) *The Parisian* isn't worth buying except for reading sensationalism.
(4) *The Parisian* isn't worth buying except to use as lavatory paper.

In the one case as in the other, the utterance is easy to interpret and the *sous-entendu* is easy to discover. The two utterances and the two *sous-entendus* are similar. However, (2) with *sous-entendu* (4) is ironical, while (1) with *sous-entendu* (3) is not. The speaker in (2) wishes to suggest broadly to his auditor: 'You and I, we both know that *The Parisian* is a paper that isn't worth reading; all it's good for is wiping one's arse.' To put it another way, (2) attracts attention to its *sous-entendu* (4), while the *sous-entendu* (3) of (1) does not attract attention, for – in the encyclopaedia of a contemporary Frenchman – it goes without saying. What the speaker is stating in (1) is surprising, while the only surprising thing about (2) is the very surprise feigned by the speaker. By the same token, while (1) evokes nothing beyond what it states, (2) is suggestive and evokes imaginary conditions in which the surprise would be real. In short, (2) participates in a symbolic use of language.

To understand how this comes about, it is necessary to consider the particular properties of the conceptual representation of utterances. Of all the ways in which an individual may provoke in another the construction of a particular conceptual representation, verbal expression is the most constraining. If someone points to a cat on a chair, there is an infinity of conceptual representations – more or less specific and differently orientated – that I can construct and that adequately describe the information to which my attention has been drawn. By contrast, if someone says to me, 'the cat is on the chair', there are very few conceptual representations that would be an adequate interpretation of the utterance. This is because the utterance directly clarifies a part of the conceptual representation that my interlocutor wished me to construct. I will complete that representation by calculating the *sous-entendus* of the utterance, that is to say, by establishing the link between the uttered statement itself and the mobilised knowledge that I tacitly share with my interlocutor.

One never makes explicit all that one wishes to convey, not because one wants to hide something, but on the contrary because on the basis of a partially explicit statement the remainder may be automatically reconstructed. Yet, precisely for that reconstruction to occur without problems, everything which is new and not self-evident must be stated, and the hearer should not be left with the effort of discovering it.

The conceptual representation of an utterance thus has a canonical form: the most immediate implications of the statement uttered contain the new information with respect to the shared knowledge of the interlocutors; the more distant implications (what are usually called presuppositions – a notion which is open to criticism and at least partly useless; see Deirdre Wilson 1973) and the *sous-entendu* correspond to already-shared information. When this correspondence between the degree of explicitness and the degree of novelty of the information is not respected, one of the conditions on conceptual representation of utterances is itself violated and the representation is put in quotes.

This being so, the difference between (1) and (2) becomes clearer. The *sous-entendu* (3) of (1) may be deduced from the encyclopaedic knowledge of contemporary Frenchmen. To speak of *The Parisian* is to invoke the image of a paper essentially devoted to sensationalism and which, for all that it may be interesting, can only be interesting as such. It thus conforms with the canonical condition that statement (3) should be left to the *sous-entendu*.

On the other hand, if one prints paper it is certainly so

that it will be read, and not so that it will be used as lavatory paper. Statement (4), far from being part of the encyclopaedia of Frenchmen is, on the contrary, paradoxical. If a speaker wishes to maintain this, he must state it directly and not leave it as a *sous-entendu*.

Now, if a speaker directly states (4) instead of merely implying it, his hearers, to make the link between their encyclopaedias and the uttered statement, must construct a *sous-entendu* such as (5):

(5) *The Parisian* isn't worth reading.

Yet, in most speech situations, the intellectual quality of a paper is more open to controversy than is the possibility of using it as lavatory paper. Therefore, to respect the canonical form, the speaker should directly state (5) and not be content to imply it.

Utterance (2) doubly violates the rules of conceptual interpretation of utterances, which establishes a direct correspondance between the degree of explicitness and the degree of informativeness (and in particular, of controversiality) of statements. The fact that *sous-entendu* (4) is more informative than utterance (2) blocks the interpretation of (2). One certainly understands the meaning of (2); one understands that (2) implies (4), but one has no way of immediately interpreting the fact that the more informative statement has only been implied. Whence we get a putting in quotes of (2) with a commentary such as that in (6):

(6) '(2)' is there to suggest (4).

But *sous-entendu* (4) cannot be linked to encyclopaedic knowledge without its own *sous-entendu* (5), and this *sous-entendu* is itself more informative than the statement that implied it. Whence we get a second putting in quotes as in (7):

(7) ' "(2)" is there to suggest (4)' is there to suggest (5).

Corresponding to this dual putting in quotes is a dual focal-isation, firstly on (4), then on (5) or, more exactly, on the fact that these statements – even though implied – are more informative than the explicit utterance that implied them, directly or indirectly. In other words, the focalisation is on the two occurrences in which the canonical condition of conceptual representation of utterances has been violated. This dual focalisation sets up two interconnected evocational fields.

We suggested that the initial aim of symbolic evocation was always to reconstruct by recollection or by imagination the background of information which, if it had been available in the active memory, would have allowed the analysis to be completed and the relevance of the defective conceptual representation to be established. Considering the example in the light of this hypothesis, we may delimit the dual evoca-tional field. The field corresponding to the focalisation of (5) comprises not only everything that the hearer knows to the discredit of *The Parisian* but also, and above all, everything that would permit consideration of this knowledge as know-ledge shared with the speaker. It is not sufficient to imagine the conditions in which (5) would be true; it is crucial to imagine the conditions in which this truth would be so evident and so evidently shared by the interlocutors that it would have been legitimate to imply it. Whence an evocation not only of all the contempt felt by some people for *The Parisian*, but also, crucially, a complicity of the interlocutors in this contempt.

The evocational field that corresponds to the focalisation of (4) comprises all that which concerns the use of news-paper as lavatory paper. On the one hand are evoked all scatological metaphors, themselves in quotes in the encyclo-paedia, that allow the expression of contempt for any object and particularly for printed paper in association with sitting and shitting; on the other hand are evoked popular mores of the countryside and the crummy bistros where *The Parisian* effectively finishes its career, hung on a nail in the lavatory. There again, this information is evoked as being self-evident, as being the object of tacit agreement between the interlocutors.

Now, even if on these points (the contemptible character of *The Parisian* and its metaphorical or actual use as lavatory paper) an agreement is possible between the interlocutors, this could be a tacit agreement only on the symbolic level. Actually, in stating that Arthur buys *The Parisian* not to put in the lavatory but apparently to read it, the speaker in (1) makes it clear that (4) is not the object of a unanimous agreement.

But what is precisely evoked by (2) in the final analysis is a tacit agreement between the speaker and hearer alone, in which others such as Arthur do not share; a complicity from which those who buy *The Parisian* either to read or to put in the lavatory are excluded. The two evocational fields linked to (4) and to (5) combine, then, to evoke the distance and the superiority of the interlocutors *vis-à-vis* both *The Parisian* and its unsophisticated public.

This example suggests three remarks:

In the first place, it shows the strict dependence between putting in quotes, focalisation, and evocation: firstly, putting in quotes is triggered by the fact that one of the conditions of conceptual representation has not been fulfilled; secondly, focalisation centres on this condition; thirdly, the evocational field comprises all the information which might enable one to conceive how this same condition would have been fulfilled.

In the second place, this example gives more substance to the hypothesis advanced in the preceding chapter according to which a representation in quotes may itself be embedded in another representation in quotes. This dual quotation results in two linked focalisations, and two overlapping evocational fields.

In the third place, this example suggests an interesting generalisation: not only irony, but all symbolic figures of language become symbolic because of a non-correspondence between, on the one hand, the degree of explicitness of the statements that enter into the conceptual representation of an utterance, and on the other, their degree of informativeness with regard to the knowledge shared by the interlocutors.

The Christian leopard and the were-hyena. The Dorze inhabit highlands which, towards the east, plunge abruptly to the wide Rift Valley and, to the west, descend more gently towards the Omo basin. All the wild animals of the area inhabit the lowlands except for two which are found in the mountains as well – the leopard and the hyena. Living at high altitude, near humans, and taking part of their food from human husbandry, these animals are already – by virtue of this exceptional character – good candidates for symbolic elaboration. Both carnivores, these two species have in other respects radically opposite habits. Leopards kill more animals than they eat, and between killing and eating a certain amount of time often elapses. Hyenas, on the contrary, eat more animals than they kill. Most of the time, they live off carrion; when they themselves kill, their prey is generally a sick or weakened animal that they start eating while it is still breathing. Such are, in Dorze eyes, some of the salient features of these two species.

It matters to the Dorze to maintain good relations with these animals that share their living-space; there are two big sacrificers who are charged with cajoling them with yearly offerings described as veritable banquets – for leopards in the one case and for hyenas in the other. To a certain extent, these species are treated like neighbouring societies. Indeed, for each neighbouring society there is a sacrificer, a lineage head, who is charged with maintaining good relations.

The leopard, as we have seen, is considered a Christian animal. He is supposed to observe the fasts of the Orthodox church, an observance which, in Ethiopia, is the principal test of faith.

The hyena is not humanised to this extent. Hyenas are thought of as having an organised social life with assemblies, rules and chiefs, but there is a tendency to do the same for all species with gregarious habits. The salient belief here does not concern the humanisation of hyenas, but, if I may put it this way, the hyenisation of some humans who are supposed to be able to turn themselves into hyenas. These *gormathe*, or were-hyenas, devour other humans, either by unearthing corpses or by eating still-living people who are generally ill. In the second instance, the victims 'see' the were-hyena come each day to devour their guts a little more, and they soon succumb in horrible suffering.

These beliefs, it will be noted, are built upon encyclopaedic knowledge. The alimentary restraint actually exhibited by leopards is simply exaggerated and structured in time as a function of the Christian ritual calendar (which the Dorze observe at the same time as their traditional rituals). The habits attributed to were-hyenas parallel the alimentary avidity of real hyenas.

Despite this encyclopaedic basis, the conceptual paradox is clear and the symbolic elaboration leaves no doubt.

Classification of living beings among the Dorze as among all the peoples of the world rests on two axioms: a species belongs to one and only one genus; an individual belongs to one and only one species. I say 'axioms' because it is not a matter of empirical truths that observations could bring into question, but of preliminary conditions for the taxonomic identification of living beings and thus for the formulation of all particular observations. Nothing suggests more clearly the symbolic character of a statement than its bringing into question – directly or by implication – these two axioms.

If leopards are Christian, this implies that they are gifted with moral qualities which, by definition, belong only to the human genus. Thus, the first axiom is contradicted. Moreover, to one species in its entirety is attributed a trait which is in no way generic: not all humans are Christians. The Dorze themselves who, it seems, were first converted in the fifteenth century, became Christian again only a few decades ago, after a long period of lack of contact with the Orthodox Empire of the north. A significant proportion of their neighbours are not Christian. For the Dorze, therefore, Christianity does not go without saying. One is not born Christian, one becomes Christian by baptism or by conversion. Christianity represents the highest degree of culture.

Yet, here are savage beasts who possess this high degree of culture and possess it naturally, simply by belonging to the leopard species. Whence the two principal paradoxes underlying this belief; leopards have as a species a moral sense that is specific to another genus; and they have as a species – that is to say, non-temporally – a religion that is, moreover, regarded as an individual or social trait acquired at a given point in time.

Were-hyenas are individuals who possess the specific traits of another species than their own, thus violating the second axiom of the classification of living beings. Moreover, just as the Christianity of the leopards is paradoxically not defined in time, the lycanthropy of were-hyenas is paradoxically not defined in space: when the were-hyena is here devouring the guts of its victim, at the same time it is there going about its daily business. And – the most important point – the two points of its ubiquity are usually distant from each other. It is not neighbours or kinsmen who are accused of being were-hyenas, but rather members of peripheral ethnic groups.

The common feature of these paradoxes is that they base a taxonomic identification on the observation of alimentary habits: leopards are restrained, and therefore they are assimilated to humans; some humans eat impure living meat or carrion, and therefore they are assimilated to hyenas. But as is shown by the irregularity of human alimentary customs, one cannot base – and even less question – a taxonomic identification on the mere fact of alimentation. Conceptual representations based on such arguments must be put in quotes. It is specifically on this taxonomic paradox that focalisation is effectuated; it is through it that the evocational field is delimited.

It is now a matter of reviewing everything that makes the alimentary morality of leopards assimilable to that of humans, Christianity assimilable to a permanent nature, the alimentary immorality of some men assimilable to a denaturation, and this denaturation assimilable to distance in space.

The belief about leopards includes in the evocational field the most valued aspects of human behaviour. The belief about were-hyenas, inversely, includes in the evocational field the most devalued aspects of this behaviour. Both situate morality on the alimentary plane. Together, they combine to evoke a symbolic characterisation of species as a function of their alimentary habits, a characterisation such that the fundamental problem is henceforth posed neither by leopards, nor by hyenas, nor by any other animal species, but by humans – who alone have irregular and variable alimentary customs in time and space.

Most peoples distinguish civilisation from savagery in meat-eating, by opposing the cooked and the raw. The Dorze, who like to eat their meat raw, stress the way in which animals are slaughtered. They must be killed by a sacrificer who only slits their throats after having thrown them down on their right sides. By contrast, all animals that die accidentally or of sickness, as well as those killed by an unqualified person or without regard for the rules, are inappropriate for consumption. Slaughtering and consumption are two stages sharply distinguished in time.

Like the Dorze, the leopard kills first and eats after. Further, it is thought to slit the throats of its prey, and only to consume those that fall on the right side. This latter belief is interesting in that it shows that, even if the Christianity of the leopard is recent as one might suppose, its humanisation is clearly ancient. The hyena, conversely, typically eats corpses that are impure because of their manner of dying, and even when it attacks living animals, it attacks them without further ceremony.

The recent re-Christianisation of the Dorze poses several problems for them. It allows them to be part of the Ethiopian entity, certainly, but only to enter it from the bottom, because their adherence is of recent date, and because they have nonetheless not renounced their traditional rituals. In these circumstances, they accentuate their Christianisation in the fifteenth century and the traces left by it: a church which had become a sacrificial place; a partial correspondence between their ritual calendar and the Christian calendar; titles such as that of *k'eso* (priest) taken from the hierarchy of titles of the Orthodox Empire. They prefer to erase the most pagan elements of their tradition and some even claim always to have fasted. In other words, without being able to deny their recent integration into the Orthodox church, they are tempted to believe that in another sense they have always been Christians – that to be Dorze means to be Christian, and always has. Now, if the leopard is Christian of its nature, the Dorze, who are no less strict than it is in their alimentary morality, can use it as the basis of an argument to evoke a more comforting image of themselves.

133

Several southern-Ethiopian peoples have alimentary customs very different from those of the Dorze. In particular, they bleed their cattle without killing them, by means of an arrow fired into the neck and quickly extracted; they consume the blood drawn in this way. It is easy to assert one's identity by contrasting oneself with these drinkers of blood. On the other hand, it is difficult to mark oneself off from the immediately neighbouring ethnic groups, the Gamo. The language, culture, mores and alimentation of the Gamo are very like those of the Dorze, but the former are not all equally Christianised. More difficult still to account for the immorality of some Dorze, if to be Dorze is to be by nature Christian.

The Dorze are quick to accuse their Gamo neighbours of being gluttons. Conversely, they accuse their own gluttons of being Gamo – false Dorze. The belief in were-hyenas, which are thought to act in Dorze country while at the same time belonging to Gamo groups, is a radical dramatisation of this theme. It suggests a rethinking of the immorality of certain Dorze as the marker of ethnic otherness. It permits the exaggeration of differences between the Dorze and the neighbouring Gamo and the relating of the latter to the yet more distant drinkers of blood. Finally, it allows the difference in culture to be seen as a difference in nature.

Nothing of all this will ever be expressly stated by a Dorze. Just as one does not insult hyenas, so one does not insult one's neighbours. The most one can do is to mock them and their gluttony. This belief allows precisely the implicit or unconscious evocation of a desire or a fear that would be scandalous if formulated explicitly: the desire to be naturally better than the neighbours and the fear of being surrounded by bad and dangerous creatures.

What do these beliefs mean? Is it necessary to repeat that they mean nothing? No; they focus the attention on the irregularity of human alimentary habits compared with those of animal species and therefore, on the impossibility of arguing from alimentary habits to generic origin. They evoke every- thing that – on the model of the Christian leopard – might enable one to see a particular alimentary ethic as a natural trait, and everything that – on the model of the were-hyenas – might enable one to see a non-respect of this ethic as hete- rogeneity or denaturation.

This example suggests three remarks: Firstly, as will have been noted, the description of it that I propose is more intuitive than is that of the preceding linguistic example. This defect results partly from the speed of its exposition – there was no question of introducing here all the ethno- graphic data that make me prefer this analysis to others which, on the face of it, would be equally plausible. This defect also results – and this is what is important – from the very nature of the material under consideration. In the case of symbolic figures of language, we have at our disposal subtle and shared intuitions about the conceptual representations of the objects of which the figurative utterance is made up. In the case of a set of beliefs and rituals, however, the under- lying conceptual representations are much less familiar. If it is clear which conditions necessitate putting these repre- sentations in quotes, we have only a very fragmentary understanding of the encyclopaedic knowledge in which the evocational field is delimited. A particular analysis can then only be substantiated indirectly, through the coherence and economy of the contribution it makes to the analysis of a cultural symbolism taken in its entirety.

It is then on purpose that I have discussed not one, but two beliefs, with regret at not being able to discuss a much larger number of them. The beliefs of any one culture are extraordinarily varied; the underlying conditions that determine their putting in quotes are already much closer to one another; finally, the evocational fields largely overlap. It is as though the different symbolic manifestations of a culture shone their light in the same direction and as though, rather than a series of distinct and poorly-lighted fields, there were a single complex field, structured by the interference of focalisations.

It may be that this concentration and this structuring of a single evocational field is only an artifact of analysis, only an hypothesis with nothing solid to support it. Yet this hypothesis is not lacking in empirical import. It comes to the following: the members of a single culture are given a range of diverse and reiterated symbolic information. This information is not directly assimilable to the encyclopaedia. No instruction, no explicit indication is given concerning the means of dealing with this information. As we have seen, exegetical commentaries (which in any case are not common to all societies) do not constitute interpretations but rather additional data to be interpreted. If individuals rejected symbolic information purely and simply, it would be impossible to see why society did not stop producing and reproducing it. One could then imagine that each individual deals with each bit of information differently. So that from the individual's point of view the symbolism of his culture would be completely heretogeneous, and from the society's point of view, individual symbolism would vary indefinitely. But if this were the case, cultural symbolism would have only a ludic function and the care taken to ensure its identity and permanence would remain unexplained.

Two possible hypotheses remain: either individuals are innately endowed with many universal constraints – with 'archetypes' that allow them to interpret every bit of symbolic information independently of every other, and always in the same way; or else – and this is the hypothesis I am defending – individuals are only endowed with a general symbolic mechanism and a learning strategy. This strategy consists, by means of focalisation, in looking for the most systematic and coherent treatment for the diverse information with which they are confronted. According to this hypothesis, the diversity of beliefs, rituals, etc., and their repetition, far from being absurd or contingent, seems necessary, for it alone makes it possible – in the absence of explicit instructions or innate schemas – to understand how the experience of cultural symbolism may lead, at least partially, to a shared orientation among the members of a single society. If this shared orientation did not exist, the very existence of cultural symbolism would remain incomprehensible.

In other words, when the evocational fields of two beliefs (such as those about Christian leopards and were-hyenas) overlap, the evocation takes place preferably in the overlapping area of the two fields and passes in review memorised information with the preferred aim of extracting from it a shared solution. The more numerous are the beliefs, rituals, etc., which are taken into account, the more the evocational field is determinate, the more restricted is the range of possible evocations, and the more the members of a single culture are led to similar evocations. At the same time – and this point is basic to an understanding of the cultural role of symbolism – the evocation is never totally determined; there always remains to the individual a considerable degree of freedom; cultural symbolism focusses the attention of the members of a single society in the same directions, determines parallel evocational fields that are structured in the same way, but leaves the individual free to effect an evocation in them as he likes. Cultural symbolism creates a commonality of interest but not of opinions, which – be it said in passing – has always troubled churchmen and politicians, manufacturers of ideology, obstinate misappropriators of symbolism.

A third remark: similar beliefs, myths, rituals are found in different and widely-separated societies or persist in a single society despite its transformations. At the same time, to interpret these symbolic phenomena completely, account must be taken of the particular circumstances in which they appear, of the encyclopaedic knowledge belonging to the society in which they develop. Whence a paradox and a systematic divergence in studies of cultural symbolism.

Often the anthropologist only studies a symbolic phenomenon from the point of view of the society in which he encounters it. He proposes an interpretation strictly linked to cultural idiosyncrasies for a phenomenon which may as well be found without these idiosyncrasies. For example, he makes his analysis of a myth dependent on the matrilineality of the society he studies, without taking any account of the fact that the same myth is found in patrilineal societies. Often, on the contrary, the anthropologist interprets the phenomenon no longer as a function of particular situations in which it is found, but as a function of other symbolic phenomena that are not necessarily found in the same situations. He thus establishes and sheds light on the generality of the phenomenon but does not explain why and how some cultures have taken it up while others have not.

The view proposed here allows the paradox to be resolved and the two approaches to be reconciled. Indeed, in cultural symbolism, the critical conditions which determine putting in quotes and focalisation result quite systematically from the very principles, from the 'axioms' on the basis of which encyclopaedic knowledge is constructed, and not from the idiosyncratic aspects of that knowledge. In the example of Christian leopards and were-hyenas, it is thus the universal principles of classification of living beings that are brought into question, and not some particular aspect of Dorze encyclopaedic knowledge. These beliefs could not be adopted in another society except as beliefs or as figures; they could not have a place in the encyclopaedia except in quotes. Further, it is this very general, or even universal, character of the conceptual conditions violated by manifestations of cultural symbolism and thus their apparent gross irrationality that explains the ease with which the anthropologist registers them (an ease which we said in the first chapter any adequate view of symbolism must explain).

The universal forms of symbolism have, then, universal critical conditions and universal focalisations. By contrast, the evocational fields determined by those focalisations differ greatly from one society to another, diverge depending on the particular point of view adopted in one society, and vary when that society changes.

Thus, the recent re-Christianisation of the Dorze on the surface only entailed a Christianisation of the belief – doubtless a very old one – in the humanness of leopards. It did not at all modify the belief in were-hyenas. It left intact the critical conditions for these beliefs and thus their focalisation. By contrast, it introduced into the evocational field a set of new data. It made evocable the intermediate situation of the Dorze between the Orthodox masters of Imperial Ethiopia and the non-Christian populations of the extreme south. The particular content of the evocational field will thus have varied in time as it may vary by societies, and by the points of view of different segments of the same society, without either the representations in quotes or the focalisations varying in the same way.

The transcultural study of symbolism has as its object the symbolic representations that are found in different cultures, their critical conditions, their focalisations, and the universal elements (or those general to a cultural area) of encyclopaedic knowledge that enter into the evocational field. The study of symbolism in a particular society may add to these first partial results and complement them by describing the idiosyncratic elements of the evocational field. Far from conflicting, if we consider these two approaches in these terms, they must necessarily go together.

Universal symbolic phenomena do not have two contradictory interpretations – the one constant and universal, the other variable and appropriate to each society; they have a universal focal structure and a variable evocational field.

The paradox that the fundamental contribution of Lévi-Strauss seemed to entail is resolved if it is considered in this perspective. Lévi-Strauss revealed as never before, the universality of focalisation and the universal elements of the evocational field in cultural symbolism. But, wishing to explain his own discoveries in semiological terms, he has, on the contrary, rendered them incomprehensible. He has in fact described neither a language nor a semantic system. The universal properties he reveals certainly exist, but they are cognitive and not semiological. Manifestations of cultural symbolism systematically violate the same universal principles of encyclopaedic knowledge so that when they seem to contrast and contradict each other, they focus all the more strongly in the same direction, they illuminate by means of the same paradoxes evocational fields with similar contours, fields into which each culture puts what it knows; fields that each individual explores according to his fears and his desires. No meaning in universal myths, but, broadly, a universal focalisation, a cultural evocational field, and an individual evocation.

Compare the three types of examples discussed in this chapter: smells that evoke actual memories; ironical utterances that evoke an imaginary complicity between speaker and hearer; beliefs that evoke a picture of the world that, were it made explicit, could only itself be put in quotes. Three completely heterogeneous objects of conceptual representation. Three evocations of completely different epistemological status. Yet, despite this heterogeneity and this difference, three times the same general structure: a putting in quotes of a defective conceptual representation; a focalisation on the condition responsible for that defectiveness; evocation in a field delimited by the focalisation.

The symbolic mechanism thus seems like a very general one that underlies extremely diverse intellectual activities. Let me make clear in what sense symbolism can be said to be both general and diverse.

The symbolic mechanism is a mental device coupled to the conceptual mechanism.

The conceptual mechanism constructs and evaluates conceptual representations by means of (1) its input – exogenous (perceptions) or endogenous (memorised information); (2) the system of semantic categories; (3) the active memory; (4) encyclopaedic entries corresponding to the semantic categories used in representations, entries that have been transferred from the passive memory to the active memory. A regularly constructed and evaluated conceptual representation is transferred to the active memory and, if need be, from the latter to the passive memory. To be more exact, it is probably not the representation itself that moves into the passive memory, but rather the trace left by the process of its construction. Conversely, conceptual representations are probably not extracted from the passive memory, but rather reconstructed by means of the traces left by previous acts of construction (see Neisser 1967). Remembering is constructive: we will soon see the importance of this point for understanding the nature of symbolic evocation.

Those conceptual representations that have failed to be regularly constructed and evaluated constitute the input to the symbolic mechanism. In other words, the symbolic mechanism has as its input the defective output of the conceptual mechanism. The symbolic mechanism deals in two stages with the defective conceptual representations that are submitted to it. Firstly, it modifies their focal structure: it shifts the attention from the statements describing the new information to the unfulfilled conditions that have made the representation defective. Secondly, it explores the passive memory in search of information capable of re-establishing the unfulfilled conditions. At the end of this process of evocation, information thus found is submitted to the conceptual mechanism which uses it together with the previously unfulfilled condition to reconstruct a new conceptual representation. The latter is the interpretation of the initial symbolic representation. The output of the symbolic mechanism thus serves as the input to the conceptual mechanism. In other words, the symbolic mechanism is a feedback device coupled to the conceptual mechanism.

This general structure holds equally well for all forms of symbolism. At the same time it allows us to state the differences among these forms and, in so far as that is necessary, to draw up a rudimentary classification of them.

Firstly, symbolic forms may be classified as a function of the initial input to the conceptual mechanism: information whose representation has been put in quotes may come from visual, auditory, olfactive, kinesthetic, etc., percepts, or from that particular class of inputs that are semantic interpretations of phonetic or graphic percepts. This classification is both the most common and the least interesting.

Secondly, symbolic forms may be classified as a function of the type of conditions that leads to putting them in quotes – that is to say, of the type of failure of the conceptual mechanism. It may be a question of a constitutional incapacity (absence of a categorisation of smells) or of a contingent incapacity (I don't understand the theory of relativity and I therefore give it a symbolic interpretation), or of a temporary fault (I don't listen to the speaker very carefully and his remarks become more evocative than instructive for me). It may be a question of an insufficiency in the construction of the representation, of a defect in the analysis (case of smells; objects poorly perceived; halos, used in the pictorial representation of supernatural apparitions; percussive sounds, whose identification follows on their perception; numbers whose conceptual representation would take a conscious effort, like the '*thousand and one* nights'; words without sense or whose sense is unknown; referential expressions without reference: 'Saint Whatnot', 'Latter Lammas', 'the King of Fools', etc.). It may be a question of an insufficiency in the evaluation of the representation, of a defect in relevance (objects made for no apparent function, like butter on the head; symbolic motivations; descriptions or stories that contradict experience; statements completely without informational content: 'It's a nice day today'; utterances that are excessively informative in the style of the Nouveau Roman; unexpected and inexplicable fortune or misfortune, etc.).

Thirdly – and this is the most interesting – symbolic forms may be classified according to the type of evocation elicited. As we have seen, evocation may be considered as the search for information that allows the re-establishment of the conceptual condition that was initially unfulfilled. Now, according to the case, the condition may be re-established by a valid representation, by an invalid representation, or by a representation that itself can neither be validated nor invalidated and that must therefore in its turn be treated symbolically. Thus in the case of smells it is only a matter of finding a recollection – that is to say a valid representation. In the case of an enigma, of a riddle or a crossword clue: the statement of the question (unlike that of an examination question) is deliberately ambiguous, figurative, without a univocal conceptual interpretation; it doesn't allow one to summon up the required information directly in the memory; but if the evocation succeeds, a valid solution is found that allows the initial question itself to be given a univocal interpretation. The evocation may end there.

In cases such as that of irony or hyperbole or of mime, the evocation ends in a solution whose only defect is that it is imaginary: it is the image of a possible world and not of the real world. But the conceptual mechanism is capable of recognising and accepting the imaginary as such. Today's possibility may become tomorrow's reality. Thus, in inter-personal relations symbolic utterances or behaviours constantly evoke what the relation may become and contribute to its transformation: the imaginary complicity evoked by irony against a third party is also an invitation to real complicity; the intensity of hyperbole is an invitation to shared enthusiasm; inversely, irony directed against the hearer, litotes, symbolic gestures of hauteur or of respect are invitations to keep one's distance. Each time, the image of what one wished the relationship to be is simply evoked and not described, and the other may respond in kind or symbolically manifest his disagreement without its ever being necessary to make his wishes explicit. All the finesse of social relationships, their intelligibility and their latitude, derive from the fact that focalisation is constraining while evocation is relatively free.

In a case such as that of the Dorze beliefs examined above, all the conceivable solutions can only be represented in quotes: to take their alimentary customs as natural is just as contrary to the very bases of Dorze encyclopaedic knowledge as it is to take the leopard for a Christian animal. In these conditions, symbolic evocation entails the construction of interpretations which are themselves symbolic and which must in their turn be interpreted, and so on, indefinitely. Starting from an initial input, the conceptual mechanism and the symbolic mechanism work in a closed loop and this goes on indefinitely until another perceptual input comes to offer a new object to the conceptual attention and thereby stops the cycle.

This infinite cyclical character, this absence of stable interpretation, is characteristic of cultural symbolism. The presence of an exegetical commentary only determines the first of a series of cycles which only end when the attention is turned elsewhere. Moreover, the repetitive side of cultural symbolism is there to set the endless evocation periodically in motion again.

The cyclical movement of cultural symbolism might seem absurd if it were not precisely for the constructive character of remembering. Indeed, it is not a question here of the endless quest for an impossible solution, but rather of a repeated work of re-organisation of the encyclopaedic memory. Each new evocation brings about a different reconstruction of old representations, weaves new links among them, integrates into the field of symbolism new information brought to it by daily life: the same rituals are enacted, but with new actors; the same myths are told, but in a changing universe, and to individuals whose social position, whose relationships with others, and whose experience have changed.

This organising and reconstructing role of the cycle is illustrated as well by the most individual form of symbolic work: the dream. When one dreams, the sensory input is almost reduced to nothing, the active memory is inhibited, and conscious control is absent. By means of an initial endogenous input (a striking recollection of the day before), or an exogenous one (a noise, a weight on the body, a call of nature), a tentative conceptual representation is constructed; but the active memory is at rest; the representation is put in quotes, i.e., symbolically treated; it evokes another, then another, and thus dream-sequences unfold not in a logical order but in one in which each evokes the following as the solution – itself problematical – of the problem it posed. As for the cognitive function of dreaming and its organising role, they are well known and it is less a question of establishing that they exist than of explaining them. I suggest that this explanation will come from a re-evaluation of symbolism itself.

It will be noted, furthermore, that if cultural symbolism and the dream in some way necessitate a long cycle, the forms apparently characterised by a short cycle, such as riddles or irony, may also, but optionally, trigger a long cycle. The solution of a riddle solves the riddle but does not solve the problem of its existence. The imaginary complicity evoked by irony may itself evoke all that is lacking to make it real. In short, an enigma evokes the enigmatic and irony as a figure evokes irony as a shared state of mind. Just as certain conceptual representations are always and necessarily symbolic, while others are symbolic only occasionally, so some symbolic representations always and necessarily trigger an indefinite evocation, while others do so only when one lends oneself to this. One should not then argue from the existence of two major types of evocation to the conclusion that they belong to radically distinct species.

Symbolic forms are various in the extreme: differing perceptual inputs, differing types of failings of the conceptual mechanism, focal conditions of all sorts, long or short cycles of evocation. May we, confronted with this variety, speak of symbolism in general? Most research on symbolism has only dealt with one or another of its aspects. The very notion of symbolism has been used to designate one property among others of the phenomena studied, and not a mechanism common to them all which would underlie all these phenomena and these alone. In short, given the essentials of previous research, it is not clear that symbolic phenomena may usefully be assembled and considered apart any more than all the oval objects in the universe, or all the bi-syllabic words in French. For some scholars, only particular aspects of symbolism possess an interesting homogeneity. For others, on the contrary, such as Cassirer or Lévi-Strauss, the interesting homogeneous ensemble is larger than symbolism as I have described it, and includes semantic categories of language as well: for them, the conceptual mechanism and the symbolic mechanism are not distinct. Similarly, when Piaget characterises symbolism, it is more as a particular tendency in the functioning of a homogeneous intellectual mechanism than as an autonomous device.

I have certainly not established the existence of a separate symbolic mechanism. The hypotheses I have put forward must be made more precise, developed further, and better substantiated. But what I hope to have established is that such a set of hypotheses, bearing on symbolism in general, is conceivable, interesting, and potentially fertile. I have tried to show that some problems (particularly those about the why and the how of the meaning of symbols) are false problems. I have tried to show that other classic problems (such as those about the relationship between belief and figure; between individual symbolism and cultural symbolism; and problems posed by the diversity of perceptual sources of symbolism; by the absence of explicit instructions guiding learning of it; by the existence of universal forms differently treated in various cultures) may be partially resolved – or at least treated in an interesting way – in the context of a cognitive perspective.

Most anthropologists are only interested in the particular properties of phenomena belonging to one culture. Anthropological theory as they see it reduces to a reasoned classification of these diverse cultural phenomena. I think, on the contrary, that anthropological theory has as its object the universal properties of human understanding, properties which, at one and the same time, make cultural variability possible and assign its limits. I have tried to disentangle the most general properties of symbolism: the particular epistemological status of the representations that express it;

the focalisation that it triggers; the evocation that accompanies that focalisation. If we take account of these general properties, if we try to understand how they fit together, the way in which particular phenomena may be described immediately changes. In a way these general properties are well known, not only by anthropologists, but even by those they study. Thus, when the Dorze like so many others accompany the statement of a belief with 'It is the custom', they expressly put this statement in quotes. When the Ndembu define a symbol as a landmark, they underline its focalising role. When Westerners speak in a vague way of meaning, they are really talking about evocation. These properties are obvious. What is not obvious is that they can be obvious, that without explicit instruction all humans learn to treat symbolically information that defies direct conceptual treatment. What underlying mechanism makes this tacit knowledge possible? When it is learned, what is the part of true acquisition and what the part of an activation of innate mental equipment? These are the fundamental questions that must be answered by a theory of symbolism.

I have not proposed such a theory here. I have tried only to define a framework within which a theory of symbolism may be constructed. To construct it is to make this framework more and more constraining, to the point where the simplicity of the hypotheses advanced here will instead seem simplistic. The aim of a metatheory is to make it both possible and necessary to go beyond it.

A scene marked my childhood: my father was seated in an armchair in the lounge, completely motionless, his hands empty, his eyes fixed on nothing. My mother whispered to me: 'Don't bother your father, he is working.'

This worked on me. Later, I too became a scholar, I went to Ethiopia as an ethnographer and I heard a Dorze mother whisper to her son: 'Don't bother your father, he is feeding the ancestors'; then I sat down on the hill from which one could see the Dorze market, but I was looking at nothing, and I was motionless. I have written this book the better to understand that work.

References

Berg, C. 1951. *The Unconscious Significance of Hair*. London.

Berlin, B. and B. Kay 1969. *Basic Color Terms*. Berkeley: University of California Press.

Borgès, J. L. 1962. *Ficciones*. New York: Grove Press.

Conklin, M. C. 1973. 'Color Categorization' in *American Anthropologist*, 75 (4).

Dell, F. 1973. *Les règles et les sons: Introduction à la phonologie générative*. Paris: Hermann.

Desmarquest, L. 1970. 'Ethnographic Notes on Ocholo'. Paris: unpublished.

Detienne, M. 1972. *Les jardins d'Adonis*. Paris: Gallimard.

Ducrot, O. and T. Todorov. 1972. *Dictionnaire encyclopédique des sciences du language*. Paris: Editions du Seuil.

Freud, S. 1963. *Introductory Lectures on Psycho-Analysis*. London: Hogarth Press.

Jakobson, R. 1960. 'Linguistics and Poetics' in T.A. Sebeok, (ed.), *Style in Language*. Cambridge, Mass.: M.I.T. Press.

Jones, E. 1967. *Papers on Psycho-Analysis*. Boston: Beacon Press.

Katz, J. J. 1972. *Semantic Theory*. New York: Harper and Row.

Leach, E. 1958. 'Magical Hair' in *Journal of the Royal Anthropological Institute*, vol. 88 (2).

1966a. 'The Legitimacy of Solomon' in *European Journal of Sociology*, vol. VII.

1966*b*. 'Virgin Birth' in *Proceedings of the Royal Anthropological Institute* (1966).

1969. *Genesis as Myth and Other Essays*. London: Jonathan Cape.

Lévi-Strauss, C. 1962. *Totemism*. Trans. R. Needham. London: Merlin Press.

1964. *Le Cru et le cuit*. Paris.

1966. *The Savage Mind*. London: Weidenfeld and Nicolson.

1968. *L'Origine des manières de table*. Paris: Plon.

1969. *The Raw and the Cooked*, vol. I. Trans. J. and D. Weightman. London: Jonathan Cape.

1971. *L'Homme nu*. Paris: Plon.

1973. *From Honey to Ashes*. Trans. J. and D. Weightman. London: Jonathan Cape.

Lévy-Bruhl, L. 1949. *Carnets*. Paris: Presses Universitaires de France.

Malinowski, B. 1926. *Myth in Primitive Psychology*. Frazer Lecture, 1925. London: Kegan Paul.

Moreno, M. M. 1935. *Favole e rime galla*. Rome: Tipografia del Senato.

Needham, R. 1972. *Belief, Language and Experience*. Oxford: Basil Blackwell.

1973. *Right and Left: Essays on Dual Symbolic Classification*. Chicago: University of Chicago Press.

Neisser, U. 1967. *Cognitive Psychology*. New York: Appleton.

Rosolato, G. 1969. *Essais sur le symbolique*. Paris: Gallimard.

Saussure, F. de. 1959. *Course in General Linguistics*. New York: Philosophical Library.

Smith, P. 1973. 'La nature des mythes' in *Diogène*, vol. 82.

Smith, P. and D. Sperber 1971. 'Mythologiques de Georges Dumézil' in *Annales E.S.C.*, vol. 26 (3–4).

Sperber, D. 1968. 'Le structuralisme en anthropologie' in *Qu'est-ce que le structuralisme?* Paris: Editions du Seuil.

1973. 'Postface' to Sperber 1968 in D. Sperber, *Le Structuralisme en anthropologie*. Paris: Editions du Seuil.

1974. 'La notion d'ainesse et ses paradoxes chez les Dorze d'Ethiopie méridionale' in *Cahiers Internationaux de Sociologie*, vol. LVI.

Todorov, T. 1972. 'Introduction à la symbolique' in *Poétique*, no. 11.

Turner, V. 1967. *The Forest of Symbols*. Ithaca, N.Y.: Cornell University Press.

1968. *The Drums of Affliction*. Oxford: Clarendon Press.

1969a. *The Ritual Process*. London: Routledge and Kegan Paul.

1969b. 'Forms of Symbolic Action' in R. F. Spencer (ed.), *Forms of Symbolic Action, Proceedings of the 1969 Spring Meeting, American Ethnological Society*. Seattle: University of Washington Press.

Wilson, D. 1973. 'Presuppositions and Non-Truth-Conditional Semantics'. Unpublished Ph.D. thesis, M.I.T.